PUT IT ON THE FRONT PAGE, PLEASE!

"The one word above all others that makes marriage successful is 'ours.'"

—ROBERT QUILLEN

PUT IT ON THE FRONT PAGE, PLEASE!

By John Henry Cutler

IVES WASHBURN, INC.
New York

FOREWARNING

By Cid Ricketts Sumner

Frankly, I was stunned. After nine months abroad, I was rejoicing to be home again and to find the children and grandchildren well and happy. Then, before I had even sat down, Bobbie thrust a newspaper at me and John stood aside watching as if I had just been handed a bomb and he wasn't sure whether it or I would blow up.

"What's this?" I said, somewhat taken aback. For the last thing I wanted at the moment was to read a paper, even if it was, as I saw at first glance, a local one, started no doubt by some foolhardy friend or neighbor with more money than brains. After my long absence, I wanted to hear family news, all the small things that never get into letters, much less into newspapers.

"Read that," Bobbie said, pointing.

I read, "John H. Cutler, Publisher and Editor." That was when I had to sit down, and quickly. "Well, well!" was all I could say. But thoughts aplenty were racing through my head. . . . Good heavens! What were they doing, starting a newspaper in Duxbury, of all places? And how in the world were they going to support it, not to mention their four children?

This was just too much. I hadn't said a word when they bought that plush new Pontiac station wagon instead of a sensible second-hand car; I'd even held my tongue when John

v

gave up a splendid, safe college position for free-lance writing, and every time I had sat down to a delicious meal in their house I had refrained from suggesting tactfully that with the mortgage payment overdue, wasn't this rather a lavish dinner they were giving me? But now ... Surely there were times when a mother and mother-in-law had a duty to speak out, regardless.

Luckily I didn't have a chance to speak for a little while, because John and Bobbie, both talking at the same time, were telling me how the notion had just struck them out of the blue, how they had plunged right in, the comical blunders they had made and what fun it all was.

I had to laugh in spite of myself, at some of their stories, even while I was thinking, "Poor dears, there's a tough time ahead of you, if you only knew it." Then it occurred to me that after all, they were young and resilient; maybe they could take it. Maybe it would be good financial discipline for them. Maybe this younger generation needed to face hard times in order to get a wise perspective of life and an appreciation of what was more important than mere comforts and conveniences—or than even a roof over their heads.

Then, as I listened, my anxiety and exasperated resignation gave way to something else. A kind of wonder came over me. They were talking as if the idea of failure had never entered their minds, and every triumph—such as someone's paying in advance for a five-dollar ad—was recounted with as much glee as if it actually amounted to something. If they were going to attempt the impossible with such spirit ... Well, it might turn out to be possible, after all; and who was I to dampen their enthusiasm? I had done a few risky things myself.

So at last I arrived at speech. *"The Duxbury Clipper,* may the wind blow fair!" And how the wind blew is told in this gay account of her courageous voyage.

vi

PUT IT ON THE
FRONT PAGE,
PLEASE!

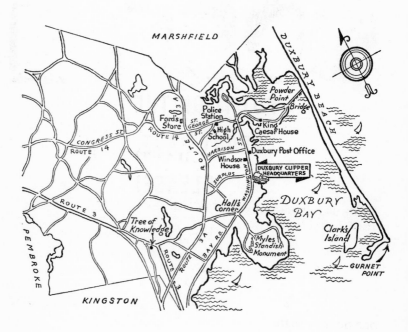

CHAPTER 1

"Why doesn't anyone ever tell us what goes on in this
confounded town?"

—HARRIED HOUSEWIFE

It all began at the bridge table
one Sunday night late in April of 1950.

I was trying to make a redoubled bid while my lovely wife,
Bobbie, a former campus queen at Cornell, was playing her
usual loquacious game of dummy. With four young children
to fend for, I was proceeding cautiously. The stakes, after all,
were a fortieth of a cent a point, and I was no Harold Vander-
bilt. That is, I couldn't play bridge as well as Harold.

Debbie was nodding briskly about something. "You are absolutely right, Bobbie. *Absolutely!* Nobody in this town ever
knows *anything* that goes on. Tonight, for instance, there was
another one of those cozy ninety-nine-cent ham-and-bean sup-

3

pers down at the First Parish Church, and George and I didn't know a blooming thing about it."

"I thought that meat loaf you served tonight was delicious," I said. "And it didn't cost me a blooming cent. Meanwhile, would you girls mind keeping it down to a college cheer while I try to play this hand?" I studied George's expression. From his smug, vulpine look, I knew he had the king of spades. When I finessed him, Debbie laid down the king and ran a string of diamonds.

"Down four redoubled vulnerable," George said cheerfully. "If you had finessed right, you would have saved yourself a quarter."

"That expression of yours," I said. "I call it cheating."

"I meant to tell you we were playing bridge, darling, not cribbage," Bobbie said. "If you keep on playing like that, you better ask Boston University for a little more money. That is, ask them to at least double your salary."

"Now, you don't have to be so sarcastic, Roberta," I said. I always call her by her given name when mildly annoyed. I reached for my pipe while George dealt the cards. "For teaching about twelve hours a week for thirty weeks a year I get $3300. Did you ever stop to figure what that means on an hourly basis? Why, even plumbers don't make that much an hour."

"I never figured your salary on an hourly basis—only on a four-children basis." Bobbie set down her cigarette after taking a meditative puff. "But that isn't what Debbie and I have been talking about. We were saying that nobody ever knows what's going on in Duxbury."

"Nonsense," George said. "Duxbury is like any other small town. Gossip rides home while the truth is asking directions."

"You men never understand," Bobbie said. "We weren't talking about gossip."

4

"Well, what were you gossiping about?" I asked.

"Debbie and I think you ought to start a little newspaper so we'll know about church suppers, PTA meetings, and all that kind of thing."

George pulled in a trick. "How can a town with a population of less than three thousand support a newspaper? A paper might get by in the summer, when all the complaints flock into town, but how about the rest of the year?"

"Well, if John doesn't start a newspaper, someone else will," Bobbie said. "Duxbury is more than three hundred years old, after all, and it's a growing community." She played a card. "He started a weekly newspaper when he was a selectee in the Army, and later, when he was with the Navy in Brazil, he was editor of the *South Atlantic News*, and that was a weekly." She stubbed out her cigarette on the ash tray. "He could do it, all right, instead of lazing around."

I was beginning to get worried, for Bobbie is one of those gals with a whim of iron. The daughter of the late Dr. James B. Sumner, a Cornell professor who had won a Nobel Prize in biochemistry three years earlier, and of Cid Ricketts Sumner, a Duxbury resident who wrote successful novels and nonfiction, she was a dynamo who didn't permit running a busy household to interfere with her activities as vice-president of the Duxbury Parent-Teachers Association, teaching Sunday school, taking lessons in tray painting, doing water colors, playing lead roles with the Duxbury Players, and entertaining at dinner any number of guests from two to forty-two. In spare moments she smocked dresses, which she sold at The Studio next door, fashioned old tablecloths into curtains, painted rooms, and never complained about not having a dishwasher. After almost ten years of marriage, I knew she never thought of failure when she raised her sights on an objective.

"The Army weekly was just a mimeographed affair," I explained, "and I had a competent staff to help put it out, including a professional cartoonist." I had dreamed up the Sixth Army Corps *Courier* as an antidote to monotony while serving in Providence, Rhode Island, after being drafted into the Army about ten months before Pearl Harbor. The West Point captain in charge of discipline had taken a dim view of the *Courier*, especially after the Providence *Journal* noted that the sassy Army publication occasionally poked fun at high brass, and contained one editorial against war. Under a subhead, "All in Fun," the *Journal* added: "More adult than most publications of the sort, this new weekly mimeographed newspaper is alert and keen and lively in flavor, and it does not hesitate to give Army bigwigs a little ribbing. Features include an advice-to-the-lovelorn column captioned 'Aunt Hattie Says.' Copies are rare in more than one sense and are not for sale. We smuggled ours out."

Debbie and Bobbie were still talking about the need for a paper.

"Just think of all the clubs and organizations we have here in town," Debbie said. "There's the Bon Homme Club, the Junior and Senior Youth Fellowship, the Tarkiln Youth Center, Barnacle Club, Rotary, Kiwanis, American Legion, and half a dozen others, including the Day and Evening Alliances."

"Whatever happened to the Afternoon Alliance?" George asked, after bidding a little slam. "Look, John," he said, "while I make this slam, why don't you bring in a round of beers?"

"With the cards we're holding," Debbie said, "it should be champagne instead of beer."

"There are a lot of other organizations in Duxbury," Bobbie said. "In fact, if you get twenty persons together in this town, they'll start a club." Her voice trailed off as I opened the door to the refrigerator. How right she was! As chairman of the float committee during the "Duxbury Days" July Fourth cele-

6

bration the year before, I had run across such social groups as the Pilgrim Daughters, the Daisy Link Club, the Duxborough Daisy Club, and the Wharf Rats, an organization much more exclusive than the Duxbury Yacht Club. Some of the tributaries of the 4-H river had such quaint names as Snip and Sew, Cream Puffer, Do It Yourself, Dainty Tid-Bits, and the Squeaky Scissors clubs. It was sometime, however, before we discovered that Duxbury had more than a hundred and twenty clubs or fraternal organizations, including a Temperance Society that must have become discouraged by the town's increasingly large cocktail parties. There was probably enough news to fill a weekly, I thought, as I poured the beer. But would there be enough advertising revenue? I put the glasses on a tray and headed for the living room.

The problem of launching a newspaper in a historic town like Duxbury was quite different from that of editing a *Courier* or a *South Atlantic News*. After serving almost nine months with the Army as a private first class in military intelligence, I had returned to my teaching duties at Dartmouth College, where I was a member of the romance languages department. Then came Pearl Harbor, and I exchanged an Army discharge for a Navy commission as lieutenant (junior grade) and wound up in Brazil after a detour at a naval air base in Kansas (where I was in charge of all Navy publications). Down in the tropics I served as historian for Fleet Air Wing Sixteen, edited the *South Atlantic News*, and gathered data on Vice Admiral Jonas Ingram, Commander of the Fourth Fleet, for an article that appeared in *Liberty* magazine under the title, "Boss of the Atlantic." Meanwhile, the former Roberta Rand Sumner, who was living across the street from Rear Admiral Richard Byrd on Beacon Hill when I met her during my tour of duty in Providence, had anchored me in

7

Duxbury by the simple expedient of buying a house. Was this an impulsive act?

"Certainly not," she said later. "I fell in love with the town the moment my family first came here in the summer of 1936."

She was reasonably sure that I could earn a living as a free-lance writer, and I felt the same way, for by the time I entered the Navy I had two syndicated columns going and had written a trunkful of features for the Boston Sunday *Post*. During my final year of service in Washington, D.C., I had been assigned to a writer unit attached to the office of the Deputy Chief of Naval Operations (for Air) and had ghosted articles and speeches for Navy officials, including Admirals Aubrey Fitch, Marc Mitscher, and Ernest King, and for Artemus Gates and John L. Sullivan. I wrote A *History of Antisubmarine Warfare in the South Atlantic* and, as a farewell assignment in collaboration with Hannibal Coons, a brief history titled *Naval Aviation in the War Against Japan*.

I had left the Navy with a deep-seated desire to continue writing, and Bobbie, with a teaching father and a writing mother, did not complain when I told her I had decided not to return to college teaching.

I thought of all these things that Sunday night in April as we drove home from the bridge game with Debbie and George.

"I mean it," she said when I turned into the driveway. "You ought to start a weekly newspaper."

"Well, let me mull over the idea," I said. Meanwhile, I tried to picture myself as the poor man's William Allen White.

CHAPTER 2

"We are returning your manuscript, which does not
quite meet our editorial requirements at this time.
Your piece is obviously too much what our readers
expect."

—THE EDITOR OF A NATIONAL MAGAZINE

Sleep was elusive that night,
and as I rolled over and over, adjusting my pillow, the events
of recent years unfolded in a confused pattern.

After being released from active duty with the Navy in
September, 1945, with the rank of lieutenant commander, I
had free-lanced and taught part-time as a "lecturer" at Boston
University. By 1950 I had written features of one kind or
another (mostly the entertainment kind) for the Boston
Transcript, Boston *Post*, Boston *Globe*, *Toronto Star Weekly*,
American Weekly, and *London Daily Mirror*.

I had turned out short pieces for *Argosy*, the *American
Magazine*, *Norte* (a South American publication), and for
Reader's Digest, along with a profile of Bill Cunningham for
Esquire, a piece titled "Women Are Wonderful But" for *Pic*
Magazine, and "Why I Quit College Teaching" for *Collier's*.
This last piece was signed "By Anonymous Ph.D." My "brain
teasers," which had made enemies for me among readers of
publications like the New York *Journal-American*, the Miami

9

Herald and other Hearst newspapers in such metropolitan centers as Norfolk, Virginia, and Chicago, Illinois, had been distributed by King Features Syndicate, and had later appeared in book form under the title *Dr. Quizzler's Mind Teasers*. I had written the first two in a series of three adventure books (my indomitable and fearless hero, Tom Stetson, operated in the Amazonian jungle of Brazil) and was working on a novel when Bobbie got her sudden inspiration about a weekly newspaper.

Adventure books . . . I suddenly thought of Tom Stetson, my blond fourteen-year-old literary godchild who hacked his way through the jungle with his Uncle Leo, a medical missionary. (One visit to the exciting zoo in Belem, Brazil, in the equatorial belt, had fired my imagination sufficiently to give mental birth to Tom Stetson.) That was exactly what Bobbie had in mind—an adventure. It would be an adventure to launch a little newspaper in a town that had gone over three hundred years without one. It was I who was timid, afraid to make a bold move. Why? I never used to be that way. I squirmed half around and batted my pillow, as if it were to blame for my sleeplessness. Some subconscious dread, maybe. Things were different, now, with a wife, and large family.

"Why don't you drink a glass of hot cocoa if you can't sleep?" Bobbie mumbled.

I went into the living room and pulled a battered old scrapbook down from a bookcase shelf. Flipping over the yellowed pages rekindled half-forgotten memories, and now I was wide awake. Two items in the scrapbook, both of which had appeared in the now defunct Boston *Transcript*, caught my eye, and I remembered them vividly as my first big newspaper thrills.

"We enjoy as a family the 'Who Is It?' feature," a physician

wrote the *Transcript* editor. "May we have information as to John H. Cutler, who he is, how come he has such an intimate knowledge of the seamy side of the personalities, is the feature syndicated, and if so, how many papers have it?"

The editor's comment: "John Henry Cutler is an instructor in Spanish at Dartmouth College with a passion for those details about the great that seem to make Napoleon and Jack Johnson of the same biological species. His collection of such details, transcribed from notes on old envelopes, tablecloths, shirt cuffs and gum wrappers, is rapidly nearing sensational proportions, and he has material to carry on his column for years to come without running out of either notables or scandals, such is the world's wealth in great men and trivia.

11

"His column is not syndicated, but made its debut and is appearing in somewhat different form in the Hanover *Gazette*.

"But let Dr. Cutler tell Dr. Davis and the numerous other readers who have expressed an interest in 'Who Is It?' something of what he is doing."

The accompanying story, under my by-line, was headed, "Cutler Comes From Behind Scrapbook to Disclose Who Is 'Who Is It?' "

I settled back on the sofa to read the second brief item, which had been published in the *Transcript* about two months later. The caption was simple: "*Transcript* Story."

"On an April morning last spring, a young man walked into the office of Alden Hoag, managing editor of the *Transcript*, with an idea for a short daily column on little known anecdotia about famous persons," the item began.

"The M.E. read several of the columns.

" 'Good stuff,' he said, 'but it lacks something to put it across. Why not write it as a question column and we'll call it 'Who Is It?' '

"It has been a regular feature of the O.E. page (opposite editorial) ever since.

"Last week, the young man, John H. Cutler, an instructor at Dartmouth, signed a contract with the United Feature Syndicate which services papers throughout the country. The *Transcript* will continue to be the only paper to carry it locally."

Soon after this notice appeared in the *Transcript*, the Hanover *Gazette* ran a story on the syndicated column. Reactions among my colleagues on the Dartmouth faculty varied.

"What do you want to be, a newspaperman or a professor?" one of them asked.

"A newspaperman," I said. By this time there was no doubt in my mind. After four years of college teaching, with raises every year, my salary was flirting with a munificent $2000. I dreamt of becoming another Westbrook Pegler or Franklin P. Adams, whose column in the *Transcript* had been displaced by my 'Who Is It?'

"In a brief six-month period," said the Hanover *Gazette*, "Dr. John H. Cutler, instructor in Spanish at Dartmouth, has rung the bell and realized the newspaper writer's dream. He has stepped from a collection of biographical odds and ends and a column in the Hanover *Gazette* to a first string feature distributed by United Feature Syndicate. His column is now taking its place across the country with such features as 'My Day' by Eleanor Roosevelt and Westbrook Pegler's 'Fair Enough.'

"Cutler, who was born thirty years ago in Boston, has acquired a Bachelor of Arts degree from Harvard, a Master of Arts and a Doctor of Philosophy from Harvard's Graduate School of Arts and Sciences, has studied at the University of the South and Middlebury College, and is now teaching French and Spanish and lecturing on the Eighteenth Century in France at Dartmouth College. The Buffalo *Evening News*, in which his column has recently been accepted, says that during his high school vacations he earned money as an iceman.

"Cutler's collection of little known facts about celebrities began as a sort of historical hobby, has been growing for years, and is now paying off."

As I riffled through the scrapbook, I wondered what would have happened to the biographical feature if the Army draft call had not hampered its production. It had been fun to skim through biographies—often as many as half a dozen a day—in search of those little-known facts which, in the aggregate, made an entertaining column, especially if the final "clue" enabled the reader to identify "Mr. X." Certainly the biggest thrill of my newspaper career came when I saw a September 1940 cover of *Editor & Publisher,* on which United Feature Syndicate had photos of "The Tops in Columnists."

As I glanced now at this cover, which was pasted in the scrapbook, I wondered how Raymond Clapper and David Lloyd George reacted when they saw my photo wedged between theirs (the arrangement was alphabetical). Journalism makes strange bedfellows, they probably thought. Nevertheless, that brief bid for fame had rekindled ambition, and it was exciting to appear on a cover with such nice folks as Eleanor Roosevelt, Drew Pearson, Robert S. Allen, Westbrook Pegler, General Hugh Johnson, and Ernie Pyle.

I put the scrapbook back on the shelf. Ironic, really. I was coming full circle. From weekly to weekly. Bobbie, I knew, was thinking of a weekly as a sort of anchor to windward—a kind of lark—not an ultimate goal. She did not mean a weekly newspaper, surely, to be a substitute for magazine articles, say, or adventure books.

For the moment, at least, I was fed up with the prospect of writing magazine pieces. Too many ups and downs! Returning from a day of teaching in Boston, I had been elated one night when my agent called from New York to say she had sold two of my articles that day. Then came famine. A national magazine, which had accepted my piece on the possible unionization of major league baseball, sent a consolation check for two hundred fifty dollars when the movement collapsed. I received the same amount from a publication of much wider circulation which had accepted, and then rejected at the last minute, a piece titled "Overweights Anonymous." When another magazine, which had kept this article for almost two months before turning it down, ran one that was quite similar, I was thoroughly disgusted. Then came the *coup de grâce*.

Another big magazine was thoughtful enough to send three inter-office memos along with a courteous rejection slip.

"An interesting idea," the first memo read.

"Could be," said the second.

The final terse comment was from the editor-in-chief: "No. Obviously too much what our readers expect."

Suddenly I was sure. Bobbie was right. It was time for another bold move, the kind of move that turns the drabness of life into adventure. And the time to start a little newspaper was in May, just before summer boom time.

CHAPTER 3

"You should like the community you choose. You are
going to live there, and become a part of it. If you
are a big-city product, and would be bored with small-
town life, don't set up shop in a rural area. You
wouldn't have your readers' best interests at heart. You
couldn't publish a paper they'd like. Your paper
wouldn't speak their language."

—A GOVERNMENT BROCHURE

By 1950, Duxbury, the oldest
summer resort in the United States, was becoming a year-
round "bedroom" community, but recreation was still its chief
industry.

From 1800 until 1850, thanks to its position as the leading
shipbuilding center in New England, Duxbury prospered.
During the romantic days of sailing ships its seafarers built
their square houses and furnished them with treasures brought

16

from East India and the Orient in ships owned by Ezra Weston, a dominant personality still remembered as "King Caesar." Ship captains built the square colonials, while the first mates were content with the simpler Cape Cods. According to Daniel Webster, who shopped for rum and other bare essentials of nineteenth-century living in Duxbury, Weston was the largest shipowner and shipbuilder in America. His vessels traded all over the world, and in his own right he was a legendary character. There was a secret passageway that led from his wharf down under the sparsoak to the cellar of his former residence, a square colonial on King Caesar Road. Behind this residence were Ezra's slave quarters, and the ancient bell which once summoned his slaves to meals still hangs in its belfry.

Duxbury's days of despair came during the latter half of the nineteenth century when sailing vessels gave way to the faster clippers and steamships. The shallowing of Duxbury harbor also contributed to the industrial gloom, and the town went broke. The bank where Daniel Webster occasionally cashed a check failed, and residents, moved to greener pastures. Duxbury was too poor to afford fancy Victorian architecture with its clutter of turrets, balconies, scroll work and gingerbread trim, thus its colonial architecture, classic in its simplicity, was preserved simply because there was no money for improvements. Today, standing behind white picket fences and lilac hedges, the renovated white Cape Cods and square colonials give the town a unique flavor that is not lost on tourists from almost every state in the Union.

Duxbury was still a ghost town when the railroad was built in the 1890's, a step toward sophistication that gave rise to the story of the tourist who asked why John and Priscilla Alden constructed their homestead so close to the railroad

17

tracks. Soon Duxbury's inns and hotels were attracting summer visitors from points as remote as California and Alaska. By 1915, water mains were installed and the town's windmills were reduced to landmarks, ending another picturesque phase. More and more people from the hinterlands were drawn to this charming rural hamlet with its sandy beaches lapped by ocean water. Along with its pine-clad hills, tree-shaded ponds and deer walks under majestic trees that protect its narrow, winding streets from sun glare, Duxbury had a history that went back to the Pilgrims.

By 1950, most of the colonials along Washington Street, the "Main Street" of the town, had been restored (some by descendants of the original settlers, others by outlanders like Bobbie and me), and the street itself had become a tourist attraction. It takes more than a tourist attraction, however, to support a weekly newspaper.

Even the main stem had few business establishments, and although there were pockets of commercial enterprises scattered around town, including a blacksmith's shop in the section called Island Creek, most of Duxbury's twenty-five square miles consisted of ponds, cranberry bogs, and woodland, with only a few sparsely settled sections. If Bobbie and I had carefully canvassed the advertising potential, we might have considered a more promising venture—opening an antique shop, for instance. Why not? We knew as much about antiques as we did about operating a weekly newspaper, and how can trafficking in old pewter, cobbler's benches, and trestle tables get you in trouble?

Soon after Bobbie decided she wanted a newspaper in the family, she found, while looking for something more literary, one of those how-to-do-it manuals in a bank in nearby Plymouth. This brochure, titled "Establishing and Operating

18

a Weekly Newspaper," was issued by bureaucrats at the United States Department of Commerce who must have gathered their data from professors of journalism. I did not read this guide to more worrisome living until 1959, as part of the research material for this book. If I had perused this excellent little treatise by early May of 1950, the *Clipper* would still be in dry dock, for it would certainly have convinced me that Duxbury was not ready for a newspaper. Also, that John Henry Cutler was not ready for a newspaper. I would not have hesitated before leaping, but, rather, would have frozen in my tracks.

For one thing, the government brochure warned of the hazards of operating a weekly in a resort area. "Unless you can be assured of making sufficient money during the boom period to carry you through the lean months, you should avoid most resort towns," said the bureaucrats. Duxbury, a small resort area, was certainly not quite the boom town that was Bar Harbor or Saratoga Springs or Newport.

Are you an editor, reporter, feature writer, circulation manager, businessman, advertising expert, promotion man? There is at least a slight implication in the brochure that if you are not all these things, you had better not try to launch a weekly. Then this note of reassurance: "But even if you are a crack Washington correspondent or a respected metropolitan city editor, you may lack the knowledge of the business and mechanical side of publishing which the weekly editor must have."

It was forunate, too, that Bobbie's mother, Cid Ricketts Sumner, had not yet written her capsule account of Duxbury for "New England Journeys," a special edition of *Ford Times* published in 1954. When Cid brought Duxbury into focus in her article, "Washington Street, Duxbury," the community did not loom as a teeming metropolis with a long line of eager advertisers clamoring for space in a weekly gazette:

It is a quiet village street two miles long, but the very essence of New England is here—history, romance, simple beauty, marvelously preserved, first by chance, now by careful design. For it was to Duxbury, Massachusetts, in about 1622 that the first settlers came from Plymouth to build summer homes and to cultivate their lands, returning in winter to the safety of the stockade.

After describing the colonial architecture that was so accidentally but happily preserved, Cid wrote:

There is only one traffic light in Duxbury, on State Highway 3A. Turn there toward the sea, round the curve and you will see the Liberty pole, so named in Revolutionary times. On your right is Blue Fish River where from 1764 to 1857 there was a quarter-mile-long wharf. The townsmen were kept busy during these times, shipping mackerel and cod. Here were launched many of the finest of the sailing vessels built by Ezra Weston . . . and his sons. The first house on the left contains the Historical Society collection, open to visitors; on the other corner is one known as the Cable Office, because when the first Atlantic cable was laid, coming in on Duxbury Beach, messages were received here.

Crossing Blue Fish River one has a fine view of the marshes, the bay and a glimpse of the outer dunes that form it. Among the stores near the post office is one over which still hangs the old sign—"Sweetser's General Store—English and West Indian Goods." Set back of the colonial with an anchor on the lawn are the world-famous Clapp Marine Biological Laboratories, open to visitors. Beyond the Congregational Church (1840) is the historic Winsor House, now run as an inn by a descendant of an early sea captain and shipbuilder of that name. One room is a replica of an English "pub" with rare prints and old muskets.

Move slowly under the arching elms. If you are held up by traffic don't honk. Lean out the window and listen—two cars have probably just stopped for conversation or to take in the family dog. It's that sort of village. Look down the short lanes that lead to the water. Many were made by ox teams hauling lumber for the ship building. Now in summer one sees white sails on the blue water.

Just beyond Surplus Street (formerly Poverty Lane) are some of the loveliest of the old houses. Farther along, set back from the road, is a large gray house once the home of Fanny Davenport, the actress. In her old carriage house is a bookshop, a good place to rest and browse.

At the flagpole in South Duxbury one may turn back toward State Highway 3A, passing the graveyard where Myles Standish is buried, or go on by the Country Way to Plymouth."

The flagpole in South Duxbury is at the center of Hall's Corner, the town's main shopping center in 1950, with two gas stations and a cluster of half a dozen stores, including a small A & P. While toying with the idea of starting a newspaper, I conducted an "advertising survey" here one Saturday morning when no experts were peeking. It was a fortnight before the first *Clipper* appeared.

Jacob Shiff, the proprietor of a modest one-roon establishment that specialized in socks, underwear, trousers and Keds sneakers, was genial and kindly. A friendly listening post for a prospective newspaper tycoon, I thought.

He was reading a Boston paper when I walked in. "Look, Mr. Shiff," I said, "if there were a weekly newspaper in Duxbury, would you advertise in it?"

"Advertise?" He set down the paper and stroked the back of his neck. "What day would it come out?"

"Does that make a difference?"

He looked surprised. "Of course. Well, if it came out on Thursday, I might."

"Every week?"

"Of course not. Certainly not every week." He smiled. "But I'll run a five-dollar ad in the first issue maybe. You know, just to help the paper get started. For five dollars I should get about a quarter of a page." He picked up a fly swatter. "What about winters? Things are pretty slow down here when the summer people go back to the city." He got the fly. "Well, anyway, I admire you for your courage."

As he went on I got the impression that anyone who dared start a newspaper in our quiet hamlet could qualify for a Purple Heart.

Next to Shiff's Store was the Marine and Appliance Company, operated by Jackson Kent. Jack, also noted for his sunny disposition, sells everything from tacks and paint remover to cabin cruisers. Would he advertise?

"Well, I don't know, John. After all, most of the boys down on the water front know we're here."

"People don't have to be taught—just reminded," I said, remembering one of Dr. Samuel Johnson's gems. "I'll bet a lot of people don't know you carry weather vanes, for instance," I said tentatively. "I didn't until just now." He still looked dubious. I had never developed an impressive sales talk, and now I wished I had listened more carefully to that last Fuller Brush man instead of practically slamming the door in his face. The only thing I remembered selling was back in grammar school days when I sat behind an orange crate on hot summer afternoons and offered diluted, but ice-cold, lemonade in clean glasses to passers-by for three cents a glass.

"Well, I'll mull it—"

Quick to detect a note of dismissal in his inflection, I talked fast. This time it was the *Reader's Digest*, not Dr. Johnson, that came to my rescue. You know—one of those little squibs which everyone reads first. "Listen, Jack. Everyone in town knows where all our churches are, don't they?"

"Sure, but what's that got—"

"If so, why do the church bells ring out every Sunday

22

morning? To remind the parishioners to come to worship, that's why. Churches have been advertising holiness for centuries." I was discouraged when he cupped a yawn. "And think what publicity has done for Pikes Peak," I said. "Did you know there are several mountains higher than Pikes Peak in Wyoming and that—"

"I thought Pikes Peak was in Colorado," Jack said. "After all the money the chamber of commerce out there has spent in advertising, do you mean to say you don't know that?"

"All right, *touché, touché*. And it's the same with Niagara Falls. There are a lot of waterfalls higher, but nobody would—"

"Excuse me while I take care of that customer over there," he said. Jack looked as if he had just been released on parole. Damn it, if Jack Kent wouldn't advertise, who would?

"Thanks, just browsing," the customer said.

"Well, I can say one thing," Jack said when he came back. "The volume of our browsing business is up this year. Okay," he added, sensing that I had another spiel ready, "I guess you can put me down for about two dollars' worth of advertising a week while your paper lasts. What are you going to call it?"

"Call it? Well, we haven't definitely decided on that point. Something dignified, I imagine, such as the *Alden Sentinel* or the *Standish Journal*. Just as long as we keep the word 'gazette' out of it, you know."

"What are your advertising rates?"

I looked toward the door, hoping a customer would come in. The question seemed almost irrelevant. Bobbie, I recalled, had phoned one weekly down on the Cape to inquire about advertising rates, but it was out of business, a victim of the boom of 1949. There was more to this newspaper business than caught the eye, that was sure. Before rates were set, we would of course have to know how much it would cost to publish a weekly. It would have to be jobbed out, naturally, since it would be too expensive to buy all the equipment needed to print it ourselves.

A customer came in, and Jack moved toward him like a retriever on the scent.

At this particular moment, unless Bobbie had just cashed a check, our bank balance was on the minus side of three hundred dollars, and not all our bills were paid. This boodle, plus a couple of hundred dollars' worth of war bonds, my salary from Boston University (I had signed up to teach summer school), and the money received from writing Boston Sunday *Post* features, would surely be enough capital to get us started. Then there was that five hundred dollars we would get early in August when I completed the boys' book called *Tom Stetson and the Blue Devil.* This jungle epic was off to a good start. That is, I had written one chapter. Jack Kent walked over after selling a paint brush.

"About our rates, Jack. I'll drop by later and give you a rate card." When we get one printed, that is, I thought. I left the store feeling our venture was off to a rather shaky start, but confident that it wouldn't always be like this. The time would come when we could say, "Oh, yes indeed. We'll have our advertising man over there the first thing in the morning."

Having completed this exhaustive advertising survey, the next problem was to find a printer. I thought of a neighbor who could give us sound advice in this connection. He lived across the street from our modest Cape Cod (it was shown on Dave Garroway's morning television program, "Today," when Duxbury's July Fourth celebration was featured in 1959). We are on the bay side of Washington Street about halfway between the two flagpoles, and opposite us, in a more imposing square captain's colonial, was Arthur ("Beanie") Beane, our oldest friend in Duxbury. Beanie, who worked for an insurance company in Boston, had something to do with preparing pamphlets telling people how long they would live. Just the person to ask about the printing and publishing business, we thought.

Beanie, who was digging in his garden, shook his head and grinned when we finished outlining Project X.

"Look, Admiral, are you out of your mind? Do you realize how much it would cost to publish a weekly newspaper and hire a staff?"

"Who needs a staff?"

"Not only that. You'll wind up with a perpetual headache. Things get pretty hectic in the printing business, even when there are no deadlines to meet."

Beanie, a great guy, has one glaring fault. He is a realist. "Seems to me you're giving up on us too easily, Beanie."

He put his spade aside and lit a cigarette. "No, don't get any ideas. I have enough problems already."

"I wasn't thinking of you so much as a partner," I said, "as an astute capitalist with both perspicuity and perspicacity. Invest four or five thousand in the *Standish Journal* and watch your money grow."

"Watch it go, you mean." He found the whole idea amusing, too fantastic for serious consideration. "You better stick to the writing end of the business."

"How much would it cost to put out a weekly?"

"I've got to run over to Kingston for some peat moss," Beanie said. "It won't hurt to stop on the way over to see Tom Porter. You know—he runs the Print Shop."

I didn't dare tell Beanie I had always thought the Print

25

Shop was a place where films were developed. "You mean we could get the paper printed right here in Duxbury?"

"I doubt it." We got into his station wagon. "Tom Porter is in his seventies, I think, and he's retired. He has a couple of linotypes, but as far as I know, all he prints are wedding invitations, posters for fairs, post cards and that sort of thing."

On the way to Elm Street, a two-mile drive, I queried Beanie about the function of a linotype. He was even more amused.

"Nice going," he said. "You want to be another Joseph Pulitzer and you don't know what a typesetting machine is. A linotype produces slugs, and each slug or casting corresponds to a line of type, get it?"

Tom Porter's two machines looked twice as retired as he did. His Print Shop was full of all kinds of mysterious-looking presses and gadgets that were all new to me. The shop, which was in a two-car garage at the end of a gravel driveway, looked as cluttered as a village hardware store in the aftermath of a hurricane, but Porter seemed to know where every last slug was.

"Those linotypes look pretty complicated," I said.

Porter patted one of them as affectionately as Gene Autry would caress his favorite horse. "This baby is an Intertype."

"I don't think my friend Beanie knows the difference between a linotype and an Intertype," I said. "Would you mind explaining?"

"Well, it's a composing machine that operates about the same as a linotype." As he rounded a few technical bends, I fell off. "You could buy a house for what this baby cost me originally," he added.

My lips were beginning to feel a little parched. Everything sounded so expensive. By this time my heart was set on publishing a weekly, but the prognosis was getting more and more negative. I recalled Beanie's words, "Do you realize how much it would cost to publish a weekly newspaper?"

"So you're thinking of starting a little news weekly, are you?" Porter was saying. He had dancing blue eyes the color of the South Atlantic, and his smile was kindly. Kindly, but with just a trace of cynicism, I thought. He jingled some coins in his pocket as he rocked back and forth on his heels.

"I was wondering whether you ever printed a weekly newspaper," I ventured. Just what he found so amusing escaped me. Maybe it was the way Beanie was grinning and shaking his head. I was beginning to feel like a museum piece.

"Did I ever print a weekly?" He kept jingling the coins, and seemed to be drifting down memory lane. "Yep, tricky things, these weeklies. I've seen them come and go. Well, I guess every city reporter dreams of owning his own little ragbag. What paper are you with?"

"None, really." Beanie looked as if he were trying to keep from sneezing. "But I've done a lot of feature work for the past ten years or so."

"I see." There was something in the way Tom Porter bent his head and rubbed his chin that suggested he was making an effort to keep a straight face. "Were you thinking of an offset throwaway or a letterpress job?"

"If you ask me," Beanie said, "he's thinking of calling the whole deal off."

"Well, I guess that's just one more little detail that has to be decided," I said. "We haven't given much thought yet to—"

"You better tell him the difference between offset and letterpress," Beanie said. He reminded me of a director of "Merton of the Movies." "As you can see, John isn't too familiar with the mechanical end of the newspaper business."

"You better stick to letterpress," Porter said after a complicated explanation of the two processes. He was jingling the coins again, and there was a faraway look in his eyes. "Well, Carl Johnson next door thinks the town needs a paper. He runs a florist shop, as you know, and he'd probably run a little ad before the holidays. I've heard Carl say he wished there was a local ragbag he could advertise in."

"Ragbag?" The steely inflection in my voice further amused Porter. "Do you think there would be enough advertisers the rest of the year, Mr. Porter? You know—when there are no holidays?"

"Yeah, that's what we used to call them," he said. "Used to be quite a few ragbags up around Dorchester way. Yep, I've seen them come and go." His last experience with a weekly, he went on, was setting type for a flourishing weekly in Plymouth, the county seat. That weekly, he said, usually had quite a few Duxbury ads. "Then, of course, there's the *Duxbury Pilgrim*."

Even Beanie thought he was joking.

"You mean you gentlemen have never heard of the *Duxbury Pilgrim?*" Porter slowly walked into the back room and returned with a newspaper about the size of the Boston papers. Sure enough, it *was* the *Duxbury Pilgrim*. Well, this was it . . . I slumped back against a counter while Porter and Beanie exchanged some gobbledegook about a change of masthead to take care of legals. While they talked, I glanced at the news items, looking for some mention of Duxbury.

"Don't look so worried, son," Porter said. "Just a few copies are printed for Duxbury legal notices. The law says legals have to be published in a local paper of circulation, but it doesn't say how big the circulation has to be. You don't see many local ads in there, do you?"

"Well, there are certainly a lot of angles to this weekly business," I said.

"Well, if it was too simple," Porter said, "every fool and his cousin would be getting into the act."

"What do you think about the advertising potential in Duxbury?" Beanie asked, as if he wanted his pessimism corroborated.

"Well, nobody will ever get rich running a weekly," Porter said.

"Don't you think Duxbury is growing pretty fast, Mr. Porter?" I asked hopefully.

He paused to light a cigarette. "Too fast to suit me. But I see what you're driving at. Won't be long before a little paper will do all right, if it can hang on." He picked up a sheet of glossy paper and folded it. "What do you think about this size? It's a little bigger than the average tabloid. Each page, except the front, would have five eighteen-inch columns."

"How many columns would the front page have?"

This time Porter thought I was kidding. Beanie almost doubled up with laughter at his look of stupefaction.

"Every page would have five columns, silly," Beanie said. "But naturally the columns on the front page would be shorter because of the masthead." He turned to Porter. "What would it cost to put out a paper this size?"

Porter turned to me. "How many pages were you thinking of?"

By this time I was too flustered to think of anything. "Oh, five or six for a starter," I said. "But that's another problem my wife and I haven't—"

"A five-pager would be a problem, all right," Porter said. "Unless you left one of the six pages blank. A six-pager, using this coated paper, would cost you $120 for twelve hundred copies and $2.50 for every additional hundred copies. An eight-pager would be $145, plus three dollars for every extra hundred."

"Suppose the paper were a little smaller," I said. "Regular tabloid size, for example, like the Boston *Daily Record*."

"Well, you wouldn't have so much room for ads. Besides, I don't have that size chase."

"Do you use solid eight-point?" Beanie asked.

Porter nodded. "And twelve-em columns."

It all sounded like double talk. As they chatted I jotted down all the technical words they used. Ems ... coigns ... galleys and galley proofs. It was a strange new vocabulary, one I would have to master unless I wanted to keep making a fool of myself. "How do you spell 'chase'?" I asked.

Tom winked at Beanie. "C–H–A–S–E." Then, noticing my embarrassment, he added. "In printing, a chase is a rectangular iron frame in which pages or columns are fastened for printing or to make plates. Don't worry, son, we'll make a printer out of you yet."

Suddenly the import of his remarks struck home. "You mean you could print the paper right here?" He nodded. I had thought the prices he mentioned were merely standard prices in the business.

"I'd have to hire a linotype operator, of course. That would mean I'd have to have cash on the line every week so I could pay the operator and the lad who's working for me now."

"Of course." With the anticipated overhead, the paper would need a lot of two- and five-dollar ads, and helpful souls like Jake Shiff and Jack Kent might be scarce.

"I was just thinking," Beanie said. "I think John should mail the first few issues free to all boxholders and RFDs, don't you, Tom? In fact, I'd keep doing that until the paper becomes a habit or John goes broke."

"It would probably be easier to break me than the habit,"

I said. "Why don't we set May 10 for the date of the first issue, which will be six pages? Well, thanks a lot, Mr. Porter. I'll bring over some copy as soon as possible."

"Fine. I'll have the masthead set up next time you come if you'll give me the name of the paper."

"What do you gentlemen think of *The Standish Journal* as a name?"

"Why not something a little more nautical?" Porter asked. "This is a seaside town, after all." He gave me a shrewd look. "How about a name like *The Duxbury Clipper?*" It was not until much later that I understood his look. It was a title Porter had discussed with another person who was thinking of starting a weekly.

The name clicked. Even Beanie was nodding favorably. A clipper was a trim, speedy craft with overhanging bow and tall raking masts that gave it graceful lines. "Sold," I said. "Well, again, many thanks, and—"

Porter pulled a little pamphlet out of a drawer. "Bring this back after you look it over. It may give you a few ideas." The title on the cover was "Country Newspaper."

While Beanie drove on to Kingston I read the brief definition of a country newspaper.

I am the friend of the family, the bringer of tidings from other friends: I speak to the home in the evening on summer's vine-clad porch or in the glow of the winter's lamp.

I help to make this evening hour; I record the great and the small, the varied acts of the days and weeks that go to make up life.

I am for and of the home; I follow those who leave humble beginnings; whether they go to greatness or to the gutter, I take to them the thrill of old days, with wholesome messages.

I speak the language of the common man; my words are fitted to his understanding. My congregation is larger than that of any church in my town; my readers are more than those in the school.

31

Young and old alike find in me stimulation, solace, comfort. I am the chronicler of man's existence.

I am the word of the week, the history of the year, the record of my community in the archives of state and nation.

I am the lives of my readers.

I am the country newspaper.

Bobbie looked up smiling when she finished reading the pamphlet. "This is going to be even more fun than I thought," she said. "I think I'll sell the Duxbury Library a subscription and suggest that bound copies be kept in the stacks."

She did, too.

CHAPTER 4

"Persons close to the newspaper field unanimously join in advising a prospective publisher to buy an existing paper rather than attempt to launch a new one."

—THAT CONFOUNDED GOVERNMENT PHAMPHLET

Almost any Duxbury resident, in 1950, unless he had moved into town within the hour, would have given the same answer to the question. "Duxbury's leading citizen? Why, Percy Walker, of course."

The late Percy L. Walker, one of the top realtors on the South Shore, was a craggy, hulking gentleman with a gray walrus mustache, a penetrating sense of humor and an uncommon ability to size up people. He didn't care how much money prospective house hunters had. If they didn't measure up to Percy's standards, he would keep showing them unattractive properties until they couldn't wait to get out of the blasted town. He went all out, however, for prospects he liked, and took them to his heart. He was a good judge of character.

"Here," he would say, as he parked his car in front of a colonial under an umbrella elm, "is one of the gems of Duxbury." Out came the biggest collection of keys in town, and Percy would lead the way in. "Nice little ship's stairway," he might say. "And that wallpaper, there ... Duxbury shell. Originated in Graham Winslow's house, they tell me." While a client probed a sagging sill, Percy would walk over to an old soapstone sink and turn on a faucet. "Nothing like good old Duxbury water." Then, to reassure a prospect who complained of the absence of a bathroom on the first floor, Percy would point to a gunstock beam and drawl, "Well, I reckon they don't build houses this way any more. Hand-adzed, these beams were. You can still see the hatchet marks." Meanwhile he would be selling Duxbury as a quaint historic community. "No place like it." He meant every word.

Percy Walker was a community leader, with the kind of vision and courage that set him apart. In an era of change, when other towns in the nation were being torn up by bulldozers, Percy stood solidly against any influence that would destroy the rural flavor of his town.

He was an oldtimer who had seen most of the important changes that had come over Duxbury, where he had been born in 1874. The Walkers were established in the area by the time of the Revolution, and when Percy married Grace Marion Delano, two old Duxbury families were united. The Delanos, unreconstructed Republicans, will admit only under

34

close questioning that they are distantly related to that upstart of a Democrat named Franklin Delano Roosevelt.

Percy Walker's wry humor and logic, along with his uncommon common sense, settled many a thorny issue at town meetings. He was the prime mover in having town water piped through Duxbury's streets in 1914, and he told us once, with a twinkle in his eye, that he did this "so people on Powder Point with windmills won't call me at night to ask me to make the wind blow."

Bobbie and I knew that here was a man who had known and loved the town from upswing days when he used to drive prospective property owners around in a horse-drawn sleigh. He knew Duxbury when you could drive around Powder Point and Standish Shore during the winter without seeing a light at night. The town changed, but Percy Walker remained the same. He was still "Mr. Duxbury."

Soon after my conversation with Tom Porter, Bobbie and I dropped by to see Percy, and were ushered onto his porch that faced the light on Route 3A. It was a strategic position that enabled Percy to see any poachers who tried to move into town. I can still see him sitting in his creaky rocker, his blue eyes piercing and perceptive under shaggy gray brows.

"So you think you want to start a little paper. H-m-m-m. . . . Well, maybe so, maybe so. . . ." Suddenly it dawned on me. Here was the Ezra Weston of modern Duxbury. A century ago anyone would have been a fool to think of launching a newspaper without consulting King Caesar.

"What do you think of the idea?" Bobbie asked.

Percy Walker, like Macaulay, was noted for his brilliant flashes of silence. He was a man who never talked unless he had something to say, unlike some of the windy orators we hear at town meeting who talk because they think they have to say something. Actually, Percy was endowed with an elo-

35

quence that could rise to any occasion, but he always knew when to brake to a stop.

"Well," he said, "guess maybe some folks would like to know what's going on in this town."

He probably could tell a lot of stories about what goes on, I thought. He and Police Chief Jimmy O'Neil have more secrets than a psychiatrist's couch.

"Since Bobbie and I are newcomers," I said, "we thought it advisable to talk things over with you." Actually, Bobbie was a newcomer emeritus, having lived in Duxbury at various times since 1936. Only acting in summer stock had interrupted some of her summers. "We'd like to ask you to be on our advisory committee." The thought struck me at that very moment. Why not have an advisory committee made up of respected citizens? Then nobody could accuse a Johnny-come-lately of trying to "change things."

"Uh-huh. . . . Well, Francis Perry is a good man. Then there's Harriet Borgeson and Elbert Harvey and Sally Dawes Chase. Douglas Pease and Walter Wrye live out there in West Duxbury." He named other distinguished townspeople, including William Wood McCarthy, the town moderator, and the late Mrs. George Putnam Metcalf, who was to write a sophisticated book review for Ye *Clipper*.

"Need a little capital, do you?"

The question, although jarring, brought smiles to our faces. We had already considered inviting one citizen of means to join our venture, but the deal fell through when he insisted on equal ownership of the paper.

"That's very nice of you, Mr. Walker," Bobbie said. "But first we'd like to see if we can get along without any help."

"H-m-m-m. . . . Well, if you do, guess maybe you could put me down for two or three hundred dollars. Have an idea Elbert Harvey might help."

"Do you think Duxbury is ready for a newspaper, Mr. Walker?" Bobbie asked. I was more concerned at the moment with whether a newspaper would be ready for Duxbury by May tenth.

He rocked back and forth for a moment. "Well, hard to say." He scratched the back of his neck. "The town thought it was ready for a railroad once. It didn't last too long."

Sensing that we took this observation to be discouraging, he bridged the awkward pause by telling a story. "I remember coming home on the train from Boston. A lady wearing a shawl kept asking Lem, the conductor, if the train stopped in Duxbury. 'Yep,' Lem kept telling her. Finally when they got down on the wooden rails, she tapped Lem on the elbow. 'You sure this train will stop in Duxbury?'

" 'Well, ma'am,' Lem said, 'if it don't, there'll be an awful splash.' "

Elbert Harvey, retired treasurer of Mount Holyoke College, was another solid citizen active in town affairs. His enthusiasm for our project made us feel as if we had picked up a four-leaf clover on the way into a casino. He would be happy, he said, to join the *Clipper* advisory board, and, yes, he thought the other prospective members were just right. He was much surer than we that some financing would be necessary.

"It will be easy enough to raise two thousand dollars or so," he said.

Two days later he told us a neighbor had informed him that if that was all the money we needed, we could borrow it from Bobbie's mother, a gracious Southerner with enough tolerance and understanding to put up with the whims of Bobbie and me. Just as generous was Bobbie's father, Professor Sumner, but as a descendant of Governor Increase Sumner and Senator Charles Sumner, he had naturally inherited some

37

of their Puritanical propriety, and who could blame him if he considered Project X ill-advised—too rash and sudden?

"Mother won't be home until some time in June," Bobbie said. She didn't add that her mother was visiting a friend in Ardross Castle (are *we* the name-dropper!), and that if she could find her way out of the two-hundred-room establishment, she *might* come home. There was always the possibility of a side trip to the Hebrides or some little fishing village in Norway, as far as Cid was concerned.

"Well, couldn't you postpone publication of your newspaper until June?" Mr. Harvey asked.

"Good heavens, no!" Bobbie said, with the kind of quiet assurance women never think needs explaining.

Mr. Harvey looked politely puzzled.

"We probably will have enough money to get started, and if we need any more, John can write a few more jungle books. Why, his plucky hero hasn't even begun to explore the Brazilian jungle!"

"And if the market for Amazon head-hunters fizzles," I said, "Bobbie plans to take in washing." I was thinking of Tom Porter and his kindly eyes. There was a man in whom I had no end of confidence. I just couldn't see Tom dunning anyone for money.

"Besides," Bobbie said, "all our relatives will subscribe to the *Clipper* for $4.50 a year. They pay more than that for *Time* or *Life*."

In the summer of 1953, when Harold Stassen, then Mutual Security Director, came to Plymouth to dedicate a replica of the first fort and meeting house, Bobbie sat beside him at luncheon. Since he was quite fascinated by her explanation of how we started the *Clipper* on a capital investment of three or four hundred dollars, we thought that you, too, dear reader, would like to know what Bobbie told Harold.

"We honestly don't have the vaguest idea, Mr. Stassen," she said.

He asked that a copy of the paper be sent to him in Washington, D.C. "Send a note with it beginning, 'Continuing our conversation about *The Duxbury Clipper*, we are sending you a copy at your request.' Then my assistants will see that I get it." He smiled. "I want to show some of my colleagues in Washington a sample of private enterprise in New England."

According to the brochure, a bit more than four hundred dollars is needed to launch a weekly, whether the purchaser jobs the paper out or acquires a plant: "The minimum capital needed to establish or purchase a weekly newspaper, every editor and publisher queried agreed, is $10,000. Most recommended $15,000."

The number of weeklies published in the United States had reached its peak in 1910, when over 16,000 were flourishing. By the late forties, half this number had been morgued. The implication was that there was a slim chance of prospering unless, of course, a primary aim was to make money. According to legend, one country editor did. He worked six days a week for sixteen hours a day for fifty years, saving almost every cent he earned. Finally he retired with $500,000 in the bank. This was a week after an uncle left him a legacy of $499,500.

"Returns to the publisher run as low as five hundred dollars net annually in cash," the brochure said. Then this optimistic note: "Other publishers, proprietors of highly successful weeklies in county seats, report incomes running well into five figures."

But Duxbury was not a county seat. It was a friendly little town where automobile drivers stopped in the middle of the road to chat while their neighbors patiently waited behind them without any honking of horns.

"What did I do that was right?" Sam Goldwyn once asked when he hit a golf ball down the middle. I asked myself the same question. Well, for one thing, I didn't read all those caveats. If so, I would have flatly told my iron-whimmed consort that since it was she, and not Duxbury, that needed a paper, she was on her own.

"And that," I certainly would have added, "is that."

CHAPTER 5

"An inexperienced man with some ready cash, who thinks he would 'like to get into the newspaper racket,' stands to lose his nest egg quickly trying to operate a weekly by himself. He probably will lose it even more quickly trying to start such a publication from scratch."

—Editor and Publisher

Bobbie and I made the jarring discovery almost at the outset that *Clipper*ing through the cross chops could be very squally indeed.

That frantic fortnight prior to publication of Volume One, Number One, is full of mercifully fading memories that still bless and burn, reminding us of the struggle to get the *Clipper* under full sail.

It was a full-time job to which we could devote only part time.

Our four bambini couldn't be completely ignored, after all. Abigail, a blonde bundle of mischief, had just turned three

41

on April Fool's Day (do you *have* to say that, Daddy?), and was too young to be stowed away in a nursery school. Meg and Dave, the brunette twins, would be seven on their mother's birthday—the Fourth of July—and they, too, were quite bouncy. Robert, the other blond, was a year older and a year noisier. Then there was our intelligent Springer, Tammy, who could woof up to ten. And Tammy woofed when his dish was empty. Did the fair Roberta have any help to ease her through the daily doleful epic of domesticity? Why, certainly, certainly. A cleaning woman came in once a week, didn't she?

To keep a few pesos flowing into the till, I wrote three or four Sunday *Post* features each week, hoping that at least two would escape the wastebasket and net me $40. Most of Monday, Wednesday, and Friday was consumed by the trip to Boston to teach five classes in French, Spanish and Portuguese, a pleasant but exacting diversion that left me physically limp and mentally frayed by the time I left the portals of Boston University in mid-afternoon. Meanwhile, the August first deadline for that stirring adventure book sequel was bedeviling me. Tom would simply have to wait in the underbrush and keep out of arrow range, unless he wanted to have his head shrunk. I had to collect news, whip it into *Clipper*ese, and get a few hours sleep each night.

Common sense would have dictated a four-pager for May 10, 1950; but for a reason still unfathomed, we had arbitrarily decided on six pages. Those extra two pages would make the sheet look more professional? Bro*ther!* If that initial effort had been as thick as *The New York Times*, it would still have borne only a slight resemblance to a newspaper. The only way to describe its format and content is to say it was a form of literature that other forms are not.

Although the first edition did not violate all the best traditions of journalism, it strove mightily in that direction. Its coated (glossy) paper was the first symptom of a novice at the tiller, as the government brochure bears witness: "As for paper, shy away from the foolish practice of printing your weekly on expensive coated stock. The price will be prohibitive. And here again habit comes into the picture. Your readers will probably have come to accept ordinary newspaper stock as standard, and will be suspicious of any attempt to use more expensive paper."

It didn't occur to Bobbie and me that coated paper was more costly than ordinary newsprint.

Mrs. Clipper was even more harassed and overworked than I. Let's tune in on this blonde thirty-two-year-old hausfrau, who interrupted her career with the Duxbury Players to concentrate on the weekly:

John was getting ready to leave for his teaching duties at Boston University. While shaving in the bathroom off our bedroom he called in: "You'd better put down that novel and get some ads. After all, the first *Clipper* is coming out in two weeks, and all we have lined up are Shiff and Kent."

" Just how do you go about getting ads?" I asked.

"You go about. Go about in your old gray Buick and tell all those merchants about the exciting new paper starting in America's home town, and that it will be mailed free to every family. Tell them it will carry no boilerplate."

"What in the world is boilerplate?" I asked.

"We'll have to look that word up. Somebody told me a country weekly should avoid the use of boilerplate, so as soon as we find out what it is we'll know what not to put in."

Boilerplate is newspaper jargon for canned items of general rather than local interest which press agents and lobbyists of one kind or another are happy to send you free.

Shortly after nine, Gail and I drove across town to Herrick Auto Sales. Although Tom was a good friend of ours, I could feel my knees shaking when I parked in front of his garage.

"What can I do for you, Bobbie?" Tom asked when he

43

came in. "A new Ford maybe? I heard that ark of yours drive up, and I think it's about ready for the last rites."

I asked whether he'd be interested in running an ad in our paper.

"Well, well, what do you know? So you are finally putting the old man to work, are you? Let me give it a little thought and I'll get in touch."

"Well, Tom, it would help if you could give me a definite idea. . . . You see, the first issue is coming out on May 10 and—"

"Are you kidding? That's not very far away, is it? How many ads have you lined up?"

"John has a couple, but you're the first person I've talked to."

While he wrote out his ad I went out and put Gail in the rear seat of the car so she couldn't get to the horn. She was getting restless, and we had scarcely started. It looked like a long morning. . . . When Tom gave me a ten-dollar ad for the front page, I was elated.

Arthur Bennett, also very friendly, ran a general store with a gas station out front. He was also postmaster in Island Creek, an old section of Duxbury, and on the side he repaired radios. Without the slightest protest he agreed to have a two-inch ad ready if I would drop in on the way back from Plymouth. Two hits in two times at bat!

I found myself humming on the way to Plymouth. After getting Gail an ice cream cone (vanilla so the stains would match her dress), I left her in the back seat with a coloring book, and went into the bank that carried our checking account. Noticing the president of the bank was busy with a client, I went into the ladies' room to comb my hair and get up a little courage. I was suddenly reminded of my freshman year at college when I tried to get an ad for the Cornell humor magazine, *The Widow*. After being rebuffed by the snarling proprietor of a candy and soda shop, I resigned and joined the dramatic club. But it was different now—a matter of bread and butter.

"Well, what can I do for you, Mrs. Cutler?" the bank president said, rearranging some papers on his desk.

44

For the first time that morning I was really jittery. I felt as if a check had bounced and I was trying to explain how it happened. He probably expected I was there for another loan, I thought, glancing at him. When I told him my mission, he went into a back room, leaving me wondering whether I should leave. I walked to the counter and picked up a copy of Banker and Tradesman. Then I noticed a booklet titled "Establishing and Operating A Weekly Newspaper." What a pleasant coincidence! It was exactly what John and I needed, I told myself as I sat down and started to read it.

"For men who have ideas, some previous experience in the field, and do not fear plenty of hard work, a modicum of opportunity awaits them in the weekly publishing field," the pamphlet said. "But the very nature of the enterprise, requiring expensive printing equipment, necessitates having considerable capital or financial backing at the start."

By the time I had finished reading this paragraph, I had decided it wouldn't be a good idea to let John read these discouraging statistics. The bank president handed me a piece of metal mounted on a block of wood. This, Tom Porter told me later, was a "cut."

"Insert this with the name of our bank, and make it look dignified," he said. "Put it in a five-dollar space." He sat down behind his desk. "Bring us a copy each week so we can leave it on the counter in case any of our customers want to read your paper."

"Thanks. I wonder whether I may borrow this booklet that tells how to start a weekly newspaper?"

For the first time he smiled. "Of course, but please return it, since others may want to read it."

During the following few days, still with Gail in tow, I toured Plymouth, Kingston, Marshfield, and Duxbury. Some persons I talked to said no politely, while others declined to advertise as if it were an affront to ask them. "All right," one storekeeper in Plymouth said, "you're a cute kid. Sign me up for a one-incher."

Some of the kindly souls who took ads had no intention of paying for them. I was crushed, after putting one delinquent in small claims court, to receive this eloquent report from the sheriff: "His next door neighbor said he took off in the dark of night and is now on the way to Florida."

I received my first jolt when I went to see George Josselyn, who ran a little variety store in the Snug Harbor section of Washington Street.

"Oh, yes," he said, after agreeing to run a one-inch "standing" ad. "I've heard about a paper starting in Duxbury."

I wasn't too surprised, because rumors in small towns are jet-propelled. I asked who had told him.

"One of my customers. Are you helping the Unitarian minister with his paper?"

"I beg your pardon?" What in the world was he talking about? "Our *Clipper* has nothing to do with the Unitarian minister," I said. We heard no more about the minister's proposed weekly newspaper until our friend Debbie filled us in. . . .

Since much of the social life of a small town is tied up with church affairs, we had invited all clergymen to send in news of coming activities, remembering that ham-and-bean supper Debbie had mentioned during our bridge game. Meanwhile, Debbie, who had mentioned the *Clipper* to the Unitarian minister, was startled by his reaction.

"I know," he said. "When I first heard about *The Duxbury Clipper* I felt like punching John Cutler in the nose." Nobody knowing the circumstances could blame him, for after almost a year of planning and consultations with a professor of journalism, he was about to launch a weekly newspaper in Duxbury. He had already engaged a linotype operator, we learned.

Another Duxbury resident had also been considering a weekly for Duxbury, unaware that anyone else had the same idea. Both prospective publishers, good sports, were among the first to wish *The Duxbury Clipper* bon voyage.

John and I solved the "resort area" problem by offering lower rates for ads that ran consecutively. Our rates run from 85¢ per column inch to $1.25, depending on frequency of insertion. This plan has worked out beautifully. Many of our clients, who prefer to insert large advertisements at certain intervals, keep a "one-incher" in the *Clipper* all the time as a "rate-holder."

My most vivid recollection of that first issue of the paper? In a jumbled haze of half-forgotten incidents, one memory stands out. It was the day the first edition was placed in the boxes at the main post office. John and I had delivered twelve hundred copies (we print almost twice that number now) to the central post office that morning at seven. At ten o'clock, when we went for our mail, it was more than exciting—it was thrilling—to watch the reactions of the townspeople, to see their surprised looks as they scanned the *Clipper*. We lingered in front of the post office listening to comments, and I recall feeling pretty proud of the sheet, and thought it looked great.

I felt that we were cheating a little, since none of the townspeople knew that John or I had anything to do with the *Clipper*. On the editorial page was the legend:

THE DUXBURY CLIPPER

Printed every Thursday by the PRINT SHOP, Elm Street
Duxbury, Massachusetts

Delivered by mail, free, to Duxbury Box Holders. Single copies ten cents at local news stands.

Advertising rates on application.

As the *Clipper* goes to press Wednesday mornings, all news copy must be received not later than noon on Tuesday. Advertising copy must be in by Monday noon. Readers are invited to send in any personal items, accounts of social functions, or reports of meetings or clubs.

Mail Address: *DUXBURY CLIPPER*, Box 43, Duxbury, Massachusetts.

It was not until the second edition of the *Clipper* appeared that we added to the legend:

John H. Cutler, Publisher and Editor

Mail subscription rates postpaid (for non-Duxbury residents): One year, $4.50; nine months, $3.50; one month, $.50 (in advance). The *Clipper* assumes no financial responsibility for typographical errors in advertisements but will reprint that part of an advertisement in which the typographical error occurs. Advertisers will please report any errors immediately.

John and I felt we were off to a propitious start, although some old-timers warned us that any newspaper would find the going rough in Duxbury. There simply wasn't enough advertising potential, they said, to support a newspaper in this tranquil hamlet by the sea.

We paid no attention to the prophets of doom and gloom, but I kept that government brochure out of John's reach. Although he knew little about navigating through the sea of weekly journalism, I was sure he would eventually make a good skipper.

Our slogan? Why, full speed ahead, of course!

CHAPTER 6

"A hick town is one where there is no place to go where
you shouldn't be."

—Robert Quillen

While the operation of every
newspaper—whether large or small, daily or weekly—is funda-
mentally the same, the basic difference between a country
weekly and a metropolitan daily is obvious. There are almost
enough people on the payroll of a big city daily to populate
a small town, whereas the full-time editorial staff of a country
weekly may be composed of only the editor and one reporter.

The operation of all newspapers boils down to the editorial
and the business functions. The editorial function consists of
the actual gathering, writing, and editing of news and other
editorial matter, which is then trimmed down into an attractive package for the reader. The business end includes the
sale of advertising space, circulation, and bookkeeping.

49

Just how did one go about getting local news, mates? As a start, Bobbie and I phoned several organizations, including the Rotary and Kiwanis clubs and the American Legion. Then came the problem of gathering news from groups we knew little or nothing about, especially those in outlying sections of town. *The Duxbury Clipper*, we agreed, would not be a Washington Street paper.

We mentioned our problems at a dinner party one night. The other guests were Betty and Peter Oldham, a charming couple who have since moved to England, where Peter was born. Peter was a jolly chap full of ideas, some of them practical. Among his suggestions for the *Clipper* was a historical column which we called "Memories of Yesterday."

"Although Duxbury was founded rather recently—not until 1637, matter of fact—it does have a dash of history," Peter said. "I know some of the social misfits who left England in the Mayflower to escape their creditors and responsibilities settled hereabouts. A column on those so-called good old days might, so to speak, titillate the literary appetites of your readers."

Peter, who regarded as Johnnies-Come-Lately any persons who had settled in England since the Norman Conquest, did not have quite the regard for the Pilgrims as did most of the old-line families of Duxbury. He reminded me of another Englishman I had met five years earlier in Washington, D.C. The incident was thus recorded in an early issue of the *Clipper*:

It was a hot July day in 1945, and the last bus had gone. While we were waiting for a taxi, a car stopped and the driver offered us a lift. There was casual conversation until the name of Duxbury was mentioned.

"I'm a bit interested in that place, you see," the driver said. The accent was as genteel as it was English. "My people came from the same ancestral home in England as the Myles Standish

50

who lived in Duxbury, Massachusetts. The name of the home was Duxbury Hall."

We asked if he was related to Myles Standish.

"Oh, yes," he said. "We are descended from the same family. And it just so happens that my name, too, is Myles Standish."

During this conversation with the English Myles Standish, I got the distinct impression that he considered the bluff soldier who came over on the *Mayflower* one of the less illustrious members of the clan.

Betty Oldham made several constructive suggestions at the dinner party, as did the hosts, Mr. and Mrs. Robert Stanton Fox. We recalled the help they and others gave us in the first anniversary issue of the *Clipper* when we thanked the happy crew that kept the *Clipper* from being scuttled during her first crossing:

Marie and Bob Fox suggested the Old English type for the masthead. Peter Oldham did the ink drawings for it and for most of the cuts, including Priscilla and John Alden, the blank anonymities of "Who Is It?" and two summer columns, "Baysides" and "Anglers' Corner," which were so crisply written, respectively, by G. Lincoln Dow and Oliver H. P. Rodman, Jr.

Grace Anthony designed the cut for her popular "Homespun Yarns" columns, which reflect the inner radiance of her mind. Betty Oldham's "Helpful Harriet" (want to get rid of that wax on your tablecloth?) also had a wide following, and at least one housewife is repapering her kitchen walls with her columns. And when it comes to birds, Betty is the John Kieran of Duxbury. She communes with them, feeds them, even has splints ready in case any of them land too hard.

Henry Cragin Walker, once on the editorial staff of the *American Magazine*, is the Thoreau of Duxbury who rises at five A.M. to enjoy life before living begins. He goes on bird walks and hikes miles along the beach. Then there is our ace reporter, Ethel McAuliffe, who does such a good job covering North and West Duxbury (and sometimes South, East and points betwixt).

51

Anne Kent and Betty Bencordo keep the school news flowing and Lorraine April is the Tarkiln Boswell. Betsy Boyd doesn't miss a thing at the Yacht Club socials and in her "Turns With a Bookworm" Margaret Metcalf keeps the beam on the best current reading. Now and then we hear from Gershom Bradford, whose knowledge of Duxbury's history is unmatched; Fisher Ames, who could also write a fascinating tome on the town's history; Mrs. W. Richmond Arnold, whose avocation as a poet surprised some of her friends; Cid Ricketts Sumner, a novelist whose first published works were poems; the late Herman Smith, whose favorite recipes we shall miss; and Neal O'Hara, the syndicated columnist.

During the first few months, the *Clipper* was hand-folded, and the list of those who came Wednesday nights includes the John Soules, the Arthur Beanes, Jr., the William Fletchers, the Glen Trimbles, the George Nelsons, the Warren Stetsons and Mr. and Mrs. Eben Phillips, Lexie Millar, and Nancy Bumpus Urquhart. The champion folders were Debbie and George, who often stayed up into the wee hours of the morning to help us meet next morning's 7:30 deadline.

A country weekly must mirror its community. Betty Oldham had this in mind when she suggested a bird column, for Duxbury, with a town forest that was virtually a bird sanctuary, and extensive woodlands shaded by towering trees, has a gorgeous variety of aerial visitors, including fox sparrows, pine and black-headed grosbeaks, towhees, brown thrashers, oven birds, hermit thrushes and red-tailed hawks. We invited readers to contribute items, and soon our subscribers heard about such rare creatures as albino robins and great snowy owls, along with kingfishers, mourning doves and handsome flickers.

Levity crept in. One reader reported seeing a morning grouse, a ruffled spouse and an extra-marital lark whose call was "Kinsey-Kinsey-Kinsey," while another explained that the call "phoe-be-be" must have come from a phoebe that stuttered. Ogden Nash, who in one bit of verse wanted to "leave no tern unstoned," might have been inspired to greater flights of fancy by *Clipper* readers who reported such mythical birds as a no left tern, a ternright, scarlet teenager, great bald ego, scowling tanager and pouter penguin.

Bobbie and I agreed the *Clipper* would be nautical but nice in tone, with a crew in lieu of a staff, and with passengers or shipmates instead of readers.

To meet the first deadline, we worked from dawn to midnight ferreting out news. Debbie was right. The town was buzzing with activity. Two church suppers were on the calendar, the Girl Scouts were working feverishly for merit badges and the Brownies made soap-bubble pipes out of spools at their last meeting. All this made small-town news. There were exhibits of flowers, water colors and tray painting around town. The Island Creek Association had a new slate of officers to announce—and names make news when they can be pegged to some such accomplishment as election to office. (We do not, however, go along with weekly editors who argue that a successful country weekly should consist of one third names.) The Day Alliance was planning an all-day sew, and the Philosophers Round Table would meet at the Unitarian parsonage for their monthly deliberation.

The town, we discovered, was full of as many alphabetical organizations as there had been in Washington, D.C., during the early days to the New Deal. Some of the combinations were mystifying to a former city lad acquainted only with the YMCA, but we finally learned to decode the WSCS, SUVCW, DNA, PTA, JYF, YPS, GFS, and the DDTS.

We kept rushing copy over to Tom Porter.

"Is this enough to fill the paper?"

Tom grinned. "It's enough if you bring in a few full-page ads. A six-page paper needs about 450 inches of type. Typescript boils down in solid eight-point, you know."

We realized what Tom meant when we saw how one story

had been condensed into two inches. A filler that was so typical of early issues when "live" news was scarce, it had been prompted by a conversation Bobbie and I had had with her aunt and grandaunt. Heading the story "Heard on Beacon Hill," we wrote:

Your roving reporter was sitting with two elderly ladies in a Beacon Hill tearoom. It was obvious that both were Proper Bostonians, but if there was any doubt of it, a remark made by one of the ladies clinched it.

"Oh, dear, I just can't seem to think of the name of that investment house down town. Not Kidder Peabody—what's the name of the other one?"

As far as Auntie May was concerned, the only two investment houses in Boston were Kidder Peabody, and Lee Higginson.

The *Clipper's* mythical "roving reporter" later became a fixture in a column called "The Oldtimer Says." Our oldtimer, who dubbed the roving reporter "Snoop-Scoop," was a salty, blunt and irreverent campfire philosopher who served us well in masked editorials. The oldtimer often blasted away at town officials or do-nothing committees while the roving reporter remonstrated with him. The feature also included Sponge, the complete oaf.

"Snoop-Scoop," the oldtimer said, "a while back Sponge asks me why I don't run for Selectman. Sponge figgers with me up there at village hall I kin give him a soft job at a hard salary. As I tell you afore, Sponge is the kind of gink what gives the word lazy a bad name."

"Well, oldtimer," the roving reporter said, "no doubt you'd make a good Selectman, but—"

"Ain't none of them fellers up there at village hall could hold a lantern to me, son, when it comes to town guv'ment. Now you take that Perry feller. Trouble is, he was three weeks old when he came to Duxbury. Now me, Snoop-Scoop, I'm a native, born and raised.

Next year I may run agin Crocker and Delano. My camp slogan will be: 'There goes the people. I must folly them, because I am their leader.' "

The oldtimer did not approve of some of the changes in Duxbury.

"Snoop-Scoop, a gink over the Point tells me they is so many folks in town, him and the missus can't give no small cocktail parties for two or three hundred folks like they used to in the gaslight days. Son, this town ain't like it was in the old days when we used to sit down in the apothecary shop over a phosphate fizz."

"I know," the reporter said. "I hear folks are trying all kinds of schemes to solve the overpopulation problem at lawn parties. One man had to hire three Boy Scouts to help find his wife at one party, it was so jammed."

The oldtimer's "It Don't Cost Very Much" committee saw that a new school in Duxbury would have no frills:

"Snoop-Scoop, we went over all the budgets and writ down every item what the sub-committees said don't cost very much. 'Why, it only costs $5000 to put this curtain on the stage,' one gink says. Then they is this bus shelter they want so the kids kin play poker while waitin' for the janitor to open the school door."

"Now, look, oldtimer, that's not fair, and—"

"They is this music room for choir practice. Why can't the kids practice in the cellar so nobody kin hear them? It's just a drop here and a dribble there, but when drops keep dribblin' you get the Johnstown Flood. Only good committee is the finance committee. When our 'It Don't Cost Very Much' committee asks these ginks for money for ink and writin' paper, you know what they say? 'Nothin' doin', it costs too much.' Them fellers is behind the ball, son."

The oldtimer disapproved of one candidate for public office. "This gink is so dumb, Snoop-Scoop, he embarrassed me somethin' awful when I take him to Bunker Hill Monument. I tell him this is where Warren fell, and you know what he

55

says? He looks up at the monument and says, 'It sure must've been a nasty fall. It killed him, I bet.' "

The roving reporter never outsmarts the oldtimer.

"Goin' to be a long, cold winter," the oldtimer said. "Worse one since the cows give ice cream a few years back."

"I suppose," your roving reporter said, "that during earthquakes your cows give whipped cream."

"Nope," he said, "buttermilk."

When Mamie, the oldtimer's wife, insisted on naming their child Clarissa, the oldtimer, holding out for Arabella, conceded defeat.

"Come to think, I like the name," he said. "First sweetheart I ever had was named Clarissa, and it will remind me of all them pleasant evenin's when we sat on the sofa and—" The oldtimer chuckled. "I kin still see Mamie. She stops dustin' and pretends to be thinkin'. Then she says, 'We'll call her Arabella. It's a more suitful name.' "

The oldtimer skewered pomposity, fraud and urbane hypocrisies. The *Clipper* itself was a frequent target (if we twitted ourselves, why should others complain if we teased them?). When someone advertised for a lost dog and offered to pay a two-dollar reward, the oldtimer explained why nobody answered the phone at the *Clipper* office:

"They were all out huntin' for the dog," he said.

The oldtimer often spoke of the good old days when it "used to rain so hard folks used two-story umbrellas," and when his neighbor "got a ticket for parkin' his yoke of oxen double." He also recalled the "earthshake that rumbled Duxbury so much the fellers up the Old Sailors' Home got seasick."

Although the oldtimer was far less grammatical than Percy Walker, he had the same wry humor and common sense, along with enough courage to stand up and be counted. We modeled him, in fact, on Mr. Walker, and I think Walker knew this. In one issue of the *Clipper* the oldtimer strongly urged taxpayers to attend a special town meeting.

"If you're not there, I'll know about it," he said. "I'll be right there sittin' in the third row."

At the meeting we watched Percy Walker stroll down the aisle. Imagine our delight when he took a seat in the third row!

Even the oldtimer could not always get voters to a meeting. One night the fire department rounded up a number of voters, but there was still no quorum. The moderator finally solved the dilemma by raiding two cocktail parties. That night everything went through without a hitch, thanks to those joyful emissaries from the gay parties.

A feature like "The Oldtimer Says" is not the only disguised editorial device a country editor can use. Gentle satire is also a powerful weapon. When no action was taken to improve the drainage on Washington Street, we inserted these paragraphs in "Sounding Off," our readers' column:

"Does that extensive lagoon I notice in front of The Studio have a name? I think it is one of the more charming ponds in New England, and wondered how the fishing and boating was."

This note was signed, "Newcomer (1883)."

Our editorial comment: "That body of water you allude to really has a bottom, contrary to rumor. Although it has no name as yet, we are conferring with The Studio about putting in a swan boat or two and possibly a couple of mallards or buffleheads. As far as we can determine there is insufficient algae to permit happy surroundings for fish."

The drainage situation was remedied.

The *Clipper*, in agreement with most committees involved in the issue, opposed building a high school on a site better

57

suited for residential development. This action, we felt, would cause traffic congestion. To get our argument across we wrote:

Saturday, P.M.—Duxbury's undefeated football team is playing Cohasset, the 1967 South Shore champions. As the band marches down historic St. George Street, which is lined on both sides with cars, candy wrappers and hot dog napkins flutter in the chill breeze as excited teenagers saunter from the concession stands to the modest new stadium. Special police officers vainly try to make children use the St. George Street overpass which the town built at great expense in 1965 to lessen traffic hazards. (There were mutinous mutters at the 1967 Town Meeting that St. George Street might have to be re-routed because of the heavy summer beach traffic while youngsters romped back and forth to the playgrounds on both sides of the street.)

The Wright Estate proponents, who reasoned that proximity to the Free Library was desirable, wonder what effect the din is having on the calm of the library. Libraries and stadia don't mix as well as ham and eggs.

Residents of St. George Street and Lover's Lane, whose requests for tax abatements were granted because their property sharply depreciated, thread their way through the traffic past the parked cars that clutter up what was once a quiet tree-shaded gateway to Duxbury proper. Duxbury has changed greatly since the $100 tax rate drove out so many residents. Efforts to bring in light industry boomeranged largely because of the prohibitive tax rate, and the one big factory that was built added nothing to the dignity of the once quaintly colonial town.

The first *Clipper*, however, and those that followed during the early months, carried no significant editorials. The first issue highlighted a controversial problem that was merely factually reported, with no editorial comment. We were lucky to have a "big story" for Volume One, Number One.

A few days before it appeared, more than three hundred embattled Duxbury residents had filled a hearing room at the State House in Boston to protest a bill that would have made a public resort area of Duxbury. The town moderator had with him a petition signed by 1165 residents. Here, now, was a nice zippy story with which to usher the newspaper age into Duxbury! We gave the State House proceedings minute coverage in the May 10 issue, reporting how a Democratic Representative had shouted that the Duxbury delegation at the hearing represented the "landed gentry" who were "members of the bloated provincial aristocracy."

The town moderator, a senior vice president of a large bank in Boston, amused the gallery with his rebuttal: "Representative Burke must have been referring to me," he said. "I started working when I was eleven, and my father started at the age of eight when he came here from Ireland. I am one of the landed gentry, too, but my property is still owned by the mortgage company."

Even this story, which filled almost a page of the *Clipper*, left yawning gaps. At wit's end, we threw in an account of the hazardous life of the Duxbury census-taker who, as he made his recent rounds, had been bitten by a dog and had been soaked three times while bicycling in the rain from door to door. One of the saddest stories we ever had to write concerned Walter Gallagher, who took this census, and a few months later was lost in his Piper Club plane. Neither his body nor that of his passenger was ever found.

Still on the prowl for local news, we focused attention on Duxbury Beach, which was making news in Boston newspapers. From Dr. Richard M. Field, a Washington Street neighbor who was former head of the geology department at Princeton University, we learned that our riviera was a sandspit (our linotype operator tried to change this to "sandpit"), not a beach, and that at its narrowest point it was only seventeen yards wide at low tide.

"You still need more copy," Tom Porter said. By this time we wished we had turned to some simpler venture, such as opening a supermarket. Was this grueling routine to continue week after week?

One more bright idea: we would localize our syndicated column, "Who Is It?" Our first "Mr. X" was Dr. William Clapp, who also lived down the street. We were familiar with his unique operations, having done a piece on him months earlier for the Boston *Sunday Post*: "Mr. X's study of marine borers has attracted scientists from all over the world, including Australia. Among his clients are the Army, Navy and Marines. . . . He never sends his customers a bill. . . ."

That column filled another ten inches, but I still had the impression that copy was disappearing into the *Clipper* like a trickle of water in a desert. Finally desperate, I threw in a Sunday supplement, even if it had little local interest.

One issue of the Boston *Sunday Post* carried six of my feature stories under five different names. Writing those pieces was ten times easier than preparing copy for that first *Clipper*.

Zero hour finally came. We were ready for the shakedown cruise.

As we stood by waiting to get under way, we wondered whether the ballast was properly laid and whether any passengers or cargo had been left at the pier. Bobbie had collected about a hundred and fifty inches of ads, not quite enough to enable us to break even. We lost almost fifty dollars on Volume One, Number One.

"In *The Duxbury Clipper*," we told readers, "there will be echoes of old Duxbury. One of the oldest towns in America, it has done more than most towns to preserve its charm and natural beauty." We invited readers to open old albums, rummage around in the attic, and examine letters yellowed with age for historic items about the town, and they enthusiastically responded.

According to the first faded newsclip received, a Cape Cod house could be built for $400 in Duxbury in 1800. In 1950, a big fireplace would cost more than that! We learned that President Grant presented the keystone of the Myles Standish Monument, which represents the United States; that Duxbury appeared on a map for the first time in 1605, when Samuel de Champlain charted Plymouth and Duxbury "by eye" as he skirted the coast. Among the hundreds of stories of old Duxbury were items with shock appeal. One reader, quoting Webster's biographical dictionary, said there was no historic basis for the tale of John Alden's proposal to Priscilla Mullens on behalf of Captain Standish as narrated in Longfellow's *The Courtship of Myles Standish*. As far as Duxbury was concerned, that was a shocking revelation, and other angry readers sent in counterblasts. We were also rebuked when we quoted an old saying: "The Pilgrim Fathers fell first on their knees and then on the aborigines." Commenting on this in a radio talk, Will Rogers remarked: "You know, one thing the Pilgrims always did was to pray, but you never saw a picture of a Pilgrim who didn't have a gun beside him. That was to see that he got what he was praying for." Will added that his ancestors didn't come over on the *Mayflower*: "They were here to meet the boat." (He was referring to his Indian ancestors, of course.)

Clipper readers liked these historical fillers. Also popular was the "Around Town" column, originally planned as another filler. A short time before Bobbie conceived the idea of the *Clipper*, I had done a Sunday *Post* feature on Winsor White of Duxbury, an authority on antiques. Remembering a recent trip he had made, I wrote the *Clipper's* first social note: "Mr. and Mrs. Winsor White returned Sunday from

61

New York, where they attended the annual White Plains Antique Show. Winsor was one of the major exhibitors of early American pieces."

"Why don't you mention Mrs. Metcalf's trip?" Bobbie asked. "She just came back from Copenhagen and Stockholm." That became "personal" number two. It was the third item in "Around Town" that almost got us into the first of the two thousand nine hundred and eighteen jams we got into later. Let's substitute "X" and "Y" for the surnames of the two families mentioned. I wrote: "Mr. William X of Brookline spent last weekend with Mrs. Frank Y during Mr. Y's absence on a business trip to New York." I caught the "Mr. William X" just in time. It should, of course, have been "Mrs. William X," who could spend a weekend with Mrs. Frank Y without arousing comment. Later the *Clipper* dropped the title "Mr." wherever possible.

Every item in the first "Around Town" column came from casual conversations with friends. "Put more of those social references in your newspaper," a friend advised. "People like to know what their neighbors are doing."

One more lesson learned. Some of the *Clipper's* social notes had more than local interest. One of Duxbury's leading citizens is Representative Francis Perry, who in 1958 was named Massachusetts Realtor of the Year by the Association of Real Estate Boards. As president of the Boston Real Estate Board, he was conferring with Mayor John Hynes of Boston about assessment practices in Boston (which Perry was instrumental in improving). Perry asked His Honor when they could meet again.

"Well, maybe we can squeeze it in next Thursday afternoon," Mayor Hynes said.

"Sorry, but I couldn't possibly make it that afternoon," Perry said. "That's when the Duxbury Board of Selectmen meet, and as a Selectman, I couldn't miss a board meeting."

The "Around Town" column is a convenient way to introduce citizens to one another. One Duxbury couple, who had attained eminence in their field, and had more degrees between them than a thermometer, were little known around town. "Confidentially," Mrs. X wrote us, "I am tired of attending cocktail parties or other social gatherings in Duxbury and overhearing someone ask, "Who are the X's—where do they come from—and so on." The *Clipper* took care of that department in its next issue.

Soon advertisers were asking to have their ads put on page three, the home of "Around Town." When that page bulged with social news and ads, the solution was simple. We spotted "Around Towners" all over the *Clipper*. Meanwhile, we charged an extra fee for ads in preferred positions. Those who wanted ads on the front page paid double rates.

Many metropolitan newspapers shy away from the practice of putting ads on the front page. Readers of country weeklies don't mind, if no significant news is left out of the paper.

In a twinkling, our readers were bombarding us with social notes—everything from births, engagements, weddings, birthday parties, to wedding anniversaries and travel notes. We learned of celebrities who were visiting Duxbury, including Fleet Admiral Chester Nimitz, Mayor William O'Dwyer of New York, and Charles Coburn, the actor.

Volume One, Number One, was to have been delivered to our home by five o'clock on Wednesday afternoon, May 9. When I returned from Boston around six that evening, Bobbie was worried.

"I don't know where the *Clippers* are," she said. "I called Tom Porter, but there's no answer."

"That calls for a martini."

63

"What calls for a martini?" Bobbie asked.

"The time, occasion and dilemma," I said. "And don't look as if you were swallowing a live eel."

She followed me into the kitchen and got the ice out while I reached for the gin. "I was amazed when Tom put the forms in the trunk compartment—"

"This sounds like the Ruth Snyder-Judd Gray murder all over again," I said. "What was Tom doing, stuffing bodies in a trunk compartment?"

"That's what they call the chases when the type is locked in," Bobbie said. "Forms." She sampled the martini when we sat in the living room. "Tom has to take the forms to Quincy to have them printed."

It was my turn to be amazed. Quincy was then about a forty-five-minute drive from Duxbury. I was so astounded I downed the entire martini, which made the Sahara seem damp by comparison. "I thought Tom said he could print the *Clipper*. You mean to tell me that with all that equipment in his shop he can't—"

"He doesn't have a newspaper press," Bobbie cut in. "There are two kinds. A rotary press and a something else. I never thought printing a little newspaper was so complicated."

"Well, it was all your idea, darling," I said.

"Right. And don't you try to take credit for it later. When and if Tom brings over the papers tonight, ask him whether we can handle mats. An advertiser wants to know."

"What did you tell the advertiser, and who was it?"

"A jeweler in Plymouth. I told him that of course we could handle mats. Now, don't get alarmed. A mat has nothing to do with rugs or carpets. I know that much. I think it's something you put in ads. Tom will know."

I pulled a dictionary down from the bookcase. A mat, I learned, was short for "matrix," a Latin word I was familiar

64

with. Matrices were pieces of cardboard which required casting into metal before they could be used in an ad. Simple.

It turned out later, however, that the mats posed another problem for Tom Porter, for he had to drive to Boston every Monday afternoon and wait a couple of hours while they were being cast. For each *Clipper*, then, Tom and his assistant had to set type, make corrections after the galley proofs were read, make up the forms, load them in his car and drive to Quincy where they were printed. Four or five hours later either Tom or one of his employees had to drive to Quincy and, if they were ready, deliver them to us to be folded for mailing.

An arduous task, printing a little weekly newspaper....

Tom Porter looked exhausted when he brought the *Clippers* over just before nine that night. I was beginning to think the routine was too rugged for a person of his age. But Tom was cheerful. "Things will work out better next week," he said.

The *Clippers* came flat, and the job of folding and collating them was long and tedious. The entire process seemed archaic in a modern robot age. All our friends, however, including Nancy Urquhart, a former Rose Bowl Queen, seemed to regard the whole thing as adventure, and some of them remained until two in the morning, when we put the papers in the Buick. By 7:30 that morning, the *Clippers* were delivered at the main post office, and by ten o'clock our first readers were glancing at Volume One, Number One. Nobody threw a *Clipper* in the wastebasket that first Thursday.

"A good augury," Bobbie said. "That's the difference between a throwaway and a giveaway." She was jubilant by evening. "The phone has been ringing all day, and everyone has had such nice things to say."

"I wonder how they found out? Maybe they called Tom Porter and asked who was putting out the paper."

"Could be." Bobbie gave me an arch look. "But I'll bet

some of the Monday Club members passed the word around."

"Don't be silly. How would anyone in the Monday Club know anything about it? We didn't call any of the gals for news."

Bobbie was smiling now. "It was at the March meeting, I think. . . . One of the girls said she wished there were a paper in town, and I told her I might talk you into starting one."

Women!

CHAPTER 7

"You will be the chronicler and historian of your community. Your most valuable asset is the confidence of your readers. They will easily detect errors, even minor ones, and will soon lose confidence in your paper if the errors are frequent, particularly if you ignore or disregard local custom and history."

—THE GOVERNMENT BROCHURE

The late John Griffin, editor of the Boston *Post,* was my favorite newspaper mentor. His editing of the mountain of copy I sent him throughout the years had taught me the value of concision. I learned to put an adjective in a noun, an adverb into a verb. I learned a writer can be concise in a volume, verbose in a line. I couldn't wait to show him the first edition of *The Duxbury Clipper.*

After glancing at it, he tapped the page-one story on the State House hearing.

"Use subheads in a long piece like this," he said. "And don't hang ads." He turned a page. "Don't island ads, either." I squirmed. Maybe I should take a course in journalism at Boston University. Why in hell was he shaking his head like that?

"Your ads should be banked," he said.

"Banked?"

"Right, banked or pyramided." From what he said I gathered that advertisements had to be inserted with some definite geographical pattern in mind, not in a willy-nilly manner.

"Ads shouldn't draw attention from your copy," he went on. "And if you bank them, each ad gets an equal place in your reader's eye."

He also cautioned against the use of clashing type faces. "Instead of splattering your pages with such a wide variety of type styles and sizes—especially in headlines—be more uniform. And some of your captions are too small. Never use ten-point unless it's an unimportant story."

I was still learning.

"You job the paper out, of course?" Griffin asked.

He grinned when I described the cumbersome procedure of putting out the paper. "Well, have fun," he said. "I know two retired reporters who tried to run a weekly, figuring there was nothing to it. One had to move out of town after going broke."

"What happened to the other? Is he still—"

"He didn't have to leave town. He just went broke."

John Griffin was not one of those hard-bitten editors who exist mostly in the popular imagination. He was friendly and simpatico, and it was because of this that his pessimistic

68

attitude had such an impact. Obviously, he did not give the *Clipper* an even chance of surviving. I had always heard that it was the dream of every newspaperman to wind up running his own sheet in a quiet little suburb, where he would be completely independent, but from Editor Griffin's comments I gathered that ownership of a weekly meant slavery, not independence.

"Your little sheet will probably keep you busy eight or nine hours a day, six or seven days a week," he said, "unless you hire a staff. And if you do that, you'll wind up working for the paper. I don't see any cuts in your *Clipper*. What are you going to do about pictures?"

"We're going to get a Polaroid camera," I said.

"Anyone around your neck of the woods with a Scanograph Engraver?" He grinned. "Never mind, John, you'll catch on. There must be a photo-engraving shop in Plymouth or Brockton. It's an expensive process, but pix are important, even in a weekly." He swiveled around, leaned back in his chair. "I suppose your editorial line will have to be straight Republican. Last time a Democrat ran for governor down in Duxbury I hear he got about fourteen votes."

"*The Duxbury Clipper* will be absolutely non-political," I said. And just why did he find this simple statement of policy so amusing?

"What are you going to do when some hot local issue comes up—go down to Duxbury Beach and bury your head in the sand? Your readers will look to you for guidance. You've got to take a stand. It's your job to clarify issues. That's what an editor is for. In small towns, where taxpayers are close to grass roots issues, you get in trouble no matter what stand you take. If you try to please everyone, you'll find you are pleasing nobody." He picked up his phone. "Drop back in a few weeks and let me know how you're doing." He cupped the receiver with his hand. "Give the thing a try. I heard of one paper that started a while back that's still in business."

That unread brochure issued by the United States Department of Commerce was more specific than John Griffin, especially in an introductory passage headed "Are You Qualified?" I certainly was not, I thought when I read the manual in 1959. Listen:

No business or profession requires more extensive general knowledge on the part of an individual. The product of the newspaperman is laid before a critical public and is subject to careful analysis. Most of the mental effort that goes into a small weekly is the product of one man. He is the newspaper. His views are the paper's. He is responsible for it morally and financially.

Do you have a wide general education? Can you write well? Are you professionally competent? Do you know what makes news, what your readers want to find in the pages of your paper? Have you an understanding of the law of libel? If you can't answer these questions in the affirmative, think twice before launching a paper.

At this point, I would have reached for the smelling salts, but those bureaucratic sadists were just warming up:

Do you have a pleasant personality? Do you like people? Are you willing to throw yourself into community work which will repay you only in good will?

The editor of a daily needs only be a good newspaperman. The weekly editor needs to be a good newspaperman and a sound businessman, since he is often editor, business manager, circulation manager, and advertising solicitor. Have you the experience and knowledge required to fill that role; the capacity for hard work? Have you good health? You'll need it.

It has been said that a weekly editor, to be a truly human journalist, must possess, in addition to his literary ability, some of the qualifications of the sociologist, psychologist, and economist.

It's a large order. Can you fill it?

Well, not *entirely*, I told myself after reading these passages. Of course I *did* take Economics A in my freshman year at college, and Social Ethics 2A as a sophomore. Who could say that these courses were not better than no preparation at all?

When I pointed out these paragraphs to Bobbie, she was horrified.

"For heaven's sake, where did you find that? We were supposed to return this booklet to the bank. I thought we had."

"Well, it was wise and just that the booklet got tucked away behind those novels of Dickens," I said. "Read this business about the qualifications of a weekly editor and you'll know precisely what I mean."

"Oh, I read all that when we started the paper," Bobbie said. "I thought it was fascinating."

"You mean you read all this stuff and—"

"Of course." She glanced at a page. "I remember this part particularly. 'Do you have a pleasant personality?' " She tossed the pamphlet on the sofa and smiled. "That's why I took over the job of advertising manager. You know how sour you can be when you take time to concentrate. I could just see you telling some advertiser who complained to go to hell. A good ad manager has to be a butter-up-erer, you know." She was still smiling. "You had a lot of things on your mind in those days. Those worries about the ups and downs of free-lancing, and all that."

"Well, all I can say is that it's lucky I didn't read this damn thing. If I had, you can bet your bottom dollar, I never—"

"I know."

"You know what?"

"I know you would have balked about launching the *Clipper*. That's why I hid the booklet. I guess I hid it so well I couldn't find it myself."

71

"The product of the newspaperman is laid before a critical public and is subject to careful analysis."
—THE GOVERNMENT BROCHURE, OF COURSE

The summer of 1950 was full of eighteen-hour working days as Mr. and Mrs. *Duxbury Clipper* sailed around in the community goldfish bowl, making mistakes for all to see. Although we learned that one did not win friends or influence readers by getting mad in print, for the public cannot tolerate a grouch, I did indulge in one polite grumble after three clubwomen and one town official told me how to run the paper:

"In Duxbury, according to our statistics, there are three Braves baseball fans, four bankers, five professors, seventeen Democrats and from three to eight thousand weekly newspaper editors, depending on the season."

Providentially, it did not occur to us at first that experts were scanning our sometimes bumbling efforts. One expert was a professor of journalism as well as a novelist, and therefore uncommonly able to detect chinks in our literary armor. The other, equally competent, was retired, which gave him ample time to find glaring errors after close scutiny. Both gentlemen, however, were gentlemen, and loosed no verbal or written barbs in our direction, despite any flaws in technique they may have found.

It would have been disconcerting had we known that just around the bend lived the night editor of the Boston *Globe* (he is now assistant managing editor). His assistant night editor, who learned the ropes on the *World-Telegram* in New York City, used to drive to Boston with him, and how they must have chuckled at some of my early journalistic bobbles!

A retired reporter from another Boston newspaper, a blustery chap who could have inflated a dirigible with one harangue, breezed into our living room one morning and graciously offered to put a little zip into the *Clipper* in return for a fee. Later he did a political column for another South Shore weekly until he was sacked. He simply didn't know the community.

We were also happily unaware of the literary connections of other Duxbury readers. One was president of a well-known publishing house in Boston. A poet who wrote books and contributed to *The New Yorker* was another reader, and we were naturally pleased when she took a winter subscription. The society editor of a Boston newspaper was another resident who subscribed to the *Clipper* when she returned to the city in the fall. "My favorite newspaper," she called our modest sheet, and that fortified our ego. We never told her publisher that she preferred our paper to his, and wasn't *that* nice of us!

"We are delighted that there is now a local paper," wrote Stuart Huckins. "Good luck." When we received his note in May we didn't know that his wife was Olga Owen Huckins, literary editor of the Boston Sunday *Post*, an example of the long arm of coincidence. (Bobbie and I were perhaps lucky Olga didn't launch a paper before we did.) Also among our readers were Ivy League college professors, non-Ivy League college professors, several teachers of English and the two

73

residents who, having given considerable thought to the idea of putting out a weekly newspaper, kept close watch on our efforts.

The "pros" could not have been blamed if they snickered at some of those early *Clippers*. There was that blazing headline in a July, 1950 issue:

TWO-MILE OCEAN MAY
COVER EARTH SOMEDAY

In smaller type was this subhead of reassurance:

But Don't Worry About It for Two
Billion Years Says Dr. Field

If any of the pros had berated us for using such a silly lead story that apparently had no local angle, our answer was ready: Dr. Richard Montgomery Field of Washington Street, former president of the American Geophysical Union, had given this scoop (only a weekly editor would be naïve enough to use this word—the pros use the term "beat") during an excursion to Woods Hole, where we were gathering data on Dr. Maurice Ewing, America's Number One oceanographer, and a former student of Dr. Field. The *Clipper* later carried our long profile of Dr. Ewing. Our excuse this time? Duxbury was a salt-water community, wasn't it? Wherefore its interest in the fascinating secrets of ocean deeps.

The pros must have wondered why in that same "Two-Mile Ocean" issue we had tucked a much newsier story away on an inside page under a ten-point head. In this footnote to history we wrote:

Daniel Mahoney, who recently visited his sister, Mrs. Theodore Berghaus of Upland Road, was waiting for a commercial plane at the Tokyo Airport when he noticed that crewmen had unwrapped General Douglas MacArthur's private plane, the *Bataan*. He wondered why at the time, for he had heard nothing of the fighting in Korea, because of strict censorship.

Half an hour after his plane left Korea word came over the radio that Southern Korea had been invaded. All planes in Tokyo were commandeered to evacuate civilians and nationals from danger zones. The plane Mr. Mahoney took was the last out of Tokyo.

Then came our first prize "typo" in the concluding paragraph:

Mr. Mahoney, who is in the woo business in Boston, has spent the past two years in Tokyo.

I was tartly informed he was in the *wool*, not the *woo*, business.

Country weeklies, which vary sharply, since they cannot help reflecting the personality of their editors, have one thing in common. They concern themselves almost exclusively with local doings. We knew this, but it took time to dredge up sufficient local news to eliminate the need of fillers that had little to do with Duxbury. Once the *Clipper* was able to navigate the channel without running aground, I told readers:

As far as a country (we said country, not hick) editor is concerned, it's more important that Ed Noyes and Bill White won the finals in a cribbage tournament than that the United States declared war on Sweden and Switzerland the same day. If Joe Stalin married Lana Turner or if Harry Truman admitted he was ever wrong, there would be no mention of it in the *Clipper*, although some may consider these things the greatest news stories since the Crucifixion. If, however, my friend Tom Lawson says, "I'd like to come to your beach party, but I have to mow my lawn this afternoon," that's news.

And so it comes to pass that some of our headlines are something less than electrifying. We dream every third night of getting that five-hundred-dollar award for the Big Story, but usually have to settle for an account of a clambake or quilting party. Headline hunting is not the concern of a country (we said country, not hick)

75

editor. We do, however, accept the what-for Neal O'Hara gave us for running a lead story on the early history of the cranberry. He told us we had set back weekly journalism a few centuries, adding: "It's all right, kid, I remember when I was struggling for recognition."

Neal O'Hara, who summered in Duxbury, does a daily "Take It From Me" stint for the Boston *Traveler*. I was pleased when he invited me to join his staff of guest columnists while he was on vacation. After all, his "guesters" included Fred Allen and John Marquand, along with the Mayor of Boston and the Governor of the Commonwealth. It was good advertising, too, to have O'Hara refer to "the erudite editor of *The Duxbury Clipper*." He knew well, however, that the little erudition I had did not include a practical knowledge of newspapering, and made several constructive suggestions. He was the first victim of one of his bits of advice.

He pointed out that a popular department in any newspaper is a reader's forum in which Mr. Enraged Taxpayer or Mrs. Outraged Citizen sends in sticks of literary dynamite. This, he said, often enlivened proceedings and aroused reader interest.

"The *Clipper*," we wrote in the tenth issue, "would welcome such contributions (i.e., comments on controversial issues). Its columns are open to the three sides every question has: your side, his side, and the correct side."

At this point the cat lay down with the pepper. Neal O'Hara found he was the Number One selection for target practice.

In guest columns I had written for him he had given me wide latitude, never objecting when I referred to him as "the poor man's Mark Twain" who "invariably arises at the crack of noon." Figuring turn about was fair play, I invited Neal to take over the "Just Between Us" column in an August issue when the tourist season was at full tide. This was a "think aloud" feature I wrote as a filler.

"Annually," he opened, "when I ask the editor of *The Duxbury Clipper* to do a guest column for me in the Boston *Traveler*, I make this assertion: 'The space is yours; say in it what you please. It will not be blue-penciled.' So, what could be more gentlemanly and equitable than for your editor to grant me the same privilege?"

Then, instead of blasting away at my inept skippering of the *Clipper*, he handed the hot end of the poker to his favorite "dislikes," including Drew Pearson: "As a courageous columnist, he pulled his neck in like a Duxbury clam when he allowed the very little man in the White House (Truman) to call him an S.O.B." Neal accused Eleanor Roosevelt of being "the first and only First Lady of the Land who commercialized her position," and pinked FDR with a few verbal quills.

Although I did not approve of Neal's comments, I did not revise them out. Then, wham! In the next issue, one of Duxbury's leading liberals, an energetic woman in her mid-eighties, let fly at O'Hara and me.

"Your readers are very much shocked and offended by O'Hara's article and also painfully surprised that you printed it. Isn't it too late—or out of date—to bring up the coarse and ill-bred comments on Mr. Roosevelt five years after the end of the 'Roosevelt hate era'? I had hoped that if the *Clipper* had any political comments to make they would be characterized by a lack of partisan bias."

Hector Holmes (brother of the Reverend John Haynes Holmes), a brilliant lawyer who lectured on patent law at Harvard Law School, also came fighting out of his corner:

"I found Mr. O'Hara's column mildly amusing (O'Hara has a national reputation as a humorist), but hardly edifying or consonant with the tone and character of your altogether charming paper. Mr. O'Hara is so gifted and can write so well it is too had he didn't give your readers something they all could enjoy."

This introductory controversy was mild compared with some of the donnybrooks that were to follow.

CHAPTER 9

"To publish a good small town newspaper is truly a Herculean task. The first prerequisite to a good paper is a good staff. Heading this staff, there must be a smart, hard working editor, who knows newspaper work inside out. And most important, the whole staff must have a deep pride in its paper."

—RICHARD LEWIS

Having written for three Boston dailies, we knew several editors and reporters on "Newspaper Row"—now a lonely landmark, since the *Transcript* and *Post* have folded and the *Globe* has moved to the most modern newspaper plant in the United States, located in South Boston. By mid-summer of 1950, my friends around Newspaper Row were inquiring about "Cutler's Folly." Their solicitude reminded me of that of a Plymouth County funeral director who was lunching in a local restaurant.

At a nearby table sat several members of a club that was one of the most exclusive of its kind. To qualify for membership, one had to be over seventy, a person of breeding and culture and of a certain religious persuasion.

"Don't put this in the *Clipper*," one member told us later, "but I must tell how amused we were last Wednesday when the funeral director came to our table and smiled. He rubbed

79

his hands and said, 'Well, gentlemen, how are you all feeling today?' There was something in his manner, cordial as it was, that gave us the impression he was thinking, 'Well, gentlemen, I wonder which one of you will be next?' "

How long would *The Duxbury Clipper* last, some of the professional newspapermen were wondering, which proves how dangerous too much knowledge can be.

Our work load was as great as ever, for after the first two issues we ran eight- and ten-page papers, which, of course, added to production costs. After paying printing, mailing and miscellaneous expenses for the first two issues, our bank balance was down to sixty-four dollars, despite the thirty-six dollars paid in advance by a few advertisers of charitable bent. Subscription money was beginning to trickle in, however, so everything seemed relatively pink and pearly. Notes that accompanied subscription checks were encouraging and flattering. A typical note: "Enclosed my check for the *Clipper*, a source of joy to me and my family. I have traveled sixteen hundred miles nearly every year since 1881 to come to Duxbury, the loveliest spot I know, and your *Clipper* will bring a touch of Duxbury to us all in the winter."

The volume of advertising in the first two editions was barely enough to support four-page papers, considering the scarcity of live news. For the third issue, we had enough advertising to justify a six-pager, but decided the *Clipper* would henceforth contain at least eight pages. Filling those pages continued to be a problem until the *Clipper* carried enough advertising to make our venture profitable. Since this required the use of more fillers, again we dug into our files, not realizing that boilerplate was boilerplate, even if it came from our files rather than from a newspaper syndicate. One example will suffice:

ALL YOU NEED IS AN IDEA

Henry Ford got the idea of mass production when he saw the principle in miniature among watchmakers. The idea for the Notre Dame backfield shift came to Knute Rockne while watching a ballet.

Walt Disney saw a mouse on the floor of his garage studio one day. It became friendly, finally climbed on his drawing board. That's how Mickey Mouse was born, first sketched on a pad of paper while Disney was traveling in an upper berth. Chopin composed his "Minute Waltz" after watching George Sand's dog chase its tail around.

Einstein says the idea of relativity came to him while he was wheeling a baby carriage in a parkway in Prague. Samuel Colt got the idea of the revolving chamber while whittling a wooden revolver. That idea revolutionized warfare.

Ah, those wonderful files, we thought. Enough material in them to entertain *Clipper* readers forever.... Then, in the first batch of "letters to the editor," came this jolt:

"Give us less general fillers and more Duxbury items."

What! Duxbury readers didn't like our wondrous collection of little-known facts? (We had used some in a column in the Boston *Globe* titled "Fun Facts.") Such items as: Richard Wagner, whose conceit was notorious, sometimes stood in front of a mirror and tipped his hat to himself, and taught his parrot to say, "Richard Wagner, you are a great man." D'Annunzio, the Italian poet, returned a letter addressed "To the greatest poet in Italy," saying, "I am not the greatest poet in Italy, I am the greatest poet in the world."

No, we learned, our readers did not. At least, they didn't like little known facts as well as local items. Samples:

Mrs. Elizabeth Mosher's taxicab was dented Tuesday when a deer rammed it while she was driving down St. George Street.

Tom Herrick, raising the hood of Sue Bradley's car in his garage yesterday, was somewhat surprised when a robin flew out and fluttered about before disappearing into the blueness of the yonder.

While an item about a bird escaping from under the hood of a car might interest a metropolitan reader as an hors d'oeuvre, it may be part of the main course in a country weekly. *Clipper* readers were interested in a one-legged sea gull which regularly perched on a buoy, and because of its excellent manners, was named Emily Post by a resident who adopted it as a pet. Once aware of this interest in sea gulls, we told our readers of a walk in the Public Garden in Boston with our seven-year-old son, Robert. Noticing the pigeons, he said, "Look, Daddy, those sea gulls are eating peanuts." Robert was clearly a shore resident.

If a candidate for the degree of Doctor of Science ever wishes to probe, in a doctoral dissertation, the lives of eccentric sea gulls, he will find ample material in back copies of the *Clipper*, including an account of a housewife who was hit by an eel as she stood on her lawn. Seeing a gull screeching high overhead, she realized the eel had slipped out of its beak. We also let our readers in on a gull secret: Herring gulls often dropped shell fish from great heights to break the shells so they could eat the succulent contents.

We told of the religious sea gull which for three consecutive Sundays perched atop the cross on the Church of Saint John the Evangelist. Although never seen there during the week, this Episcopalian gull reported regularly at its aerial station for three Sunday mornings, and left immediately after church services. When it did not return, the rector shrugged. "Probably didn't like my last sermon," he said.

Another resident, casting for stripers, boated a sea gull hooked on a bass lure, and neighbors down the street, recently brought up a sea gull hatched from an egg found on Clark's Island in Duxbury Harbor.

As the weeks passed, we discovered literary talent in town and were delighted when certain residents offered to write a weekly column on a Duxbury theme. Our columns for bird watchers, fishermen and sailors were going strong when Grace Anthony, a minister's wife, dropped in and asked whether the *Clipper* could use another feature.

"Well, I'd like to glance over a few columns before deciding," I said, trying to look editorial. Those were the words John Griffin used that morning many moons ago when, after accepting my first offering, I asked whether he was interested in more. I had always thought of Mrs. William Anthony as a person of great piety and charm, not as a writer. The *Clipper* already carried a lot of church news, and since some readers were not Episcopalian, there might be mutinous muttering if Mrs. Anthony's column became a fixture. Baptists, Catholics, Methodists, Nazarenes and Unitarians might ask for equal space. Soon the *Clipper*, awash with parables from the Old and New Testaments, would be too celestial in tone for the average reader who went to church only once a week. If Grace Anthony writes a column, won't it be too pious?

Well, she did and it wasn't. "Homespun Yarns" by Grace Anthony warmed the hearts of *Clipper* readers, especially women, for it was full of whimsy and flavored with the typical comments of a harried housewife with four children.

Other gifted writers sent in copy that a metropolitan editor would have paid for gladly. Herman Smith, formerly gourmet editor of *The American Home,* and author of *Kitchens Near and Far* and *Stina,* wrote delightful pieces for the *Clipper* and contributed a weekly recipe, unfailingly delicious.

Mrs. W. Richmond Arnold, known to the readers of the Boston *Herald*'s society column as Alison Arnold, set a high standard for nostalgic articles when she wrote "Long Ago Duxbury" for an early issue. She followed with another headed, "That's How It Was in 1907."

One elderly resident, who traces his family back past the time of the *Mayflower*, collared us and indignantly asked why we permitted such an article to appear:

"Why, she has been living in Duxbury only about forty years," he said. "What in the devil does she know about the town?"

This resident was only slightly more impressed when Miss Sadie Paulding, who retired from the Duxbury school system after fifty years of devoted service, penned another account of Duxbury under the caption "That's How It Was in 1904."

The trend continued. Dr. Alice Bigelow, whose prose was masterful, told readers what Duxbury was like in the 1890's, and Gershom Bradford, brother of Laurence Bradford (author of a history of Duxbury), also revived old days with the magic of his prose. Another favorite writer was the late Mary Nye Gifford, who wrote "That's How It Was in the 1870's."

Mrs. George Putnam Metcalf, who owned a bookshop and wrote poetry, contributed "Turns with a Bookworm" each week. Readers learned that when she reviewed Charles Flood's novel, *Love Is a Bridge*, in the *Clipper*, she received this note from him:

DEAR MARGARET METCALF:
I have only just recently received from the clipping service the reviews of my novel, *Love Is a Bridge*, and I had not seen your review published in *The Duxbury Clipper*. I thought it was one of the best reviews on the book in the whole country. . . . I am up in Maine at the moment, working on another novel, and finding there is nothing like being snowed in with a typewriter to get results. . . .

Another popular columnist was Henry Cragin Walker, who loved to arise at five in the morning and walk down to the beach. His column, "Through the Looking Glass," dwelt on the theme that the best things in Duxbury were free. In one column, he irked a local clam digger, and we thought we would have a libel suit to contend with.

"Clams are still scarce here," wrote Walker, "but Joe X, a clam digger, says they are coming back. In August, when tides are low, Joe gets in two diggings a day; he has a radio in his dory for entertainment."

The radio detail annoyed Joe X. He thought it ridiculed him.

Walker regaled his readers with such items as:

"Bees, feeding on rotten apples, often get drunk from imbibing the alcohol they obtain. They wobble about, unable to fly, a lesson to humans who drink too freely."

"Deer cross your path in Duxbury. I have seen at High Pines raccoons, wild rabbits, and foxes. You will also find in Duxbury woodchucks, quail, pheasants, snakes and eagles. I once saw a fish-hawk teaching her young to dive at low tide."

"Mrs. Leonard Johnson kicked at a hose in her garden and it moved. It turned out to be a black snake about three feet long."

"About twenty years ago, I saw three small whales, weighing about four hundred pounds each. They were towed out to sea where they sank."

Walker's mention of wild life brought other reports from readers, some amusing and unusual. A housewife said she saw a "Mama skunk crossing the road followed by five little skunks in single file. Mama's head was stuck in a small glass jar. I let her pass and she disappeared in the tall grass, but I must confess that my conscience has troubled me since. What would you have done?"

"Written off the glass jar as a total loss," I said.

Dr. William Clapp was experimenting with snakes when an eight-foot gopher snake disappeared. An elderly woman, hearing about it, phoned him: "Is it true that one of your snakes has escaped?"

"Yes," he said, "but it's harmless."

"Would it eat a cat?"

"No, but a cat might eat it."

It seemed that her cat had vanished. Both cat and snake, completely undigested, turned up. The gopher snake was found coiled up in the doorway of Josselyn's Store. "Business," the proprietor said, "was never worse than that morning."

Ian Gordon, an author staying in Duxbury, contributed dramatic reviews, and Cid Ricketts Sumner brightened our pages. Nevertheless *The Duxbury Clipper* had a long way to go before it could call itself a newspaper.

In June of 1950 we received a letter addressed to *Old Duxbury Skipper Magazine,* from a resident of East Northfield, Massachusetts!

DEAR SKIPPER:

While attending the 75th anniversary of Smith College, my alma mater, I heard about your new magazine from Duxbury friends, and this seemed to be what I was looking for, at least from hearsay.

I come of a long line of Cape Cod stock and can be pretty salty on occasion. My great-grandfather, Amaziah Atwood, was a sea captain out of Wellfleet in the early 1800's; my grandfather established, with a partner, the first wholesale fish business on Atlantic Avenue in Boston. I have collected notes on the early fishing industry, but have never had leisure to put them in shape for publication.... I am enclosing my Nantucket interview with an old-timer who would not divulge his name. The article, titled "Nantucket—Then and Now," might be changed to "A Couple of Goofs at Nantucket," if you care to use it in your magazine.

Our magazine, indeed! She had a nerve, calling our little newspaper a magazine....

Another item came from James Garfield, grandson of President James B. Garfield. James, who had an office on State Street in Boston, wrote:

Dr. Marvin Baty sent me a copy of your *Clipper* in which you ask about the houses that my father and I formerly owned in Duxbury. My father, Harry A. Garfield, was president of Williams College. He first lived in the little cottage on King Caesar Road which is the second house beyond the Old Sailors' Home. Later he sold that house and lived in the house subsequently sold to Dr. Baty.

My own house, in which we spent ten summers, was recently purchased by Mr. Hamilton Edwards on Powder Point Avenue....

As these excerpts indicate, early *Clippers* were sedate. The first item that generated gasps came from a reader who reported in "Sounding Off:"

Henry Cragin Walker strolls along the beach too early to see arresting sights. Spotted recently late one sun-splashed afternoon was a photographer taking pictures of a nude behind a sand dune.

87

"Printer's gremlins are little imps of Satan that infest a print shop and hide typographical errors until it's too late to do anything about them. Just to illustrate how easy it is for them to do their work you can figure that there are about 30 individual letters and spaces in each of these lines. Each requires a mechanical operation. If for any reason one of these operations fails you have an error in that line. . . . It is easy to see the number of chances of error are fantastic just in one line, even when you have the right letters and spaces. Multiply that by 2,560 and you have the approximate chances of mechanical error in an average issue of your favorite weekly newspaper. Of course this doesn't include the advertisements."

—THE MARLINTON (W. VA.) JOURNAL

A country editor—call him Jones—received this note from a correspondent:

Every time I send you a write-up about our Missionary society meeting you get it all balled up so it doesn't make sense. Time and again I've sent in corrections, but you get them mixed up, too. So I give up. In the future when I send you our Missionary society write-up, please don't print it.

We have received a generous quota of "Dear Sir You Cur" epistles from equally irate correspondents.

At one baby shower we listed twenty matrons who were

88

"guests of honor," implying, of course, that all these lovely ladies were big with child. In a legal notice we had an esteemed and austere citizen requesting "permission to hell," an ambition quite out of character for this pillar of the church. (The word was sell, not hell.)

All was harmony until this ad appeared:

FOR COOKING and light house work Fridays & Saturdays 10 A.M. until after dinner call 673 eves.

The lady of the manor who inserted this advertisement was deluged with telephone calls. I was deluged by one phone call from her.

"I wanted a *cook*," she said, "not a situation cooking."

Poor me. All I did was leave out the initial word "Wanted."

When the *Clipper* reported that a lad in West Duxbury had "the groppe," a reader asked whether this new disease was contagious, and a high school senior sent in a sizzling reminder that her name was "Patty," not "Potty." (Had she been less hefty, our error might have been ignored.) Then there was the surname of a friend that came out "Burp," which brought a comment all the way from Buffalo.

Mistakes which pass unobserved in the metropolitan press are more conspicuous in a closely read home-town paper as we learned when we reported that a woman was recuperating from "a broken keg." Did the keg break and fall on her, or did she try to recover the contents of a keg that broke we were asked. Look, we told one wiseacre, all the gal did was break a leg. He wanted to know if that wasn't enough.

"I advertised for a light housekeeper, not a lighthouse keeper," a housewife complained.

A weekly editor must spell names correctly. He should not print "Elburt" for "Elbert." For months we had confused two families, Mr. and Mrs. George L. Peirce and Mr. and Mrs.

George A. Pierce. When this was called to our attention, we tried to rectify the error. The correction came out: "In a recent issue we confused the George Pierwces with—" but why go on? Those confounded gremlins, again, who also accounted for our mention of "the Garthur Odfrey show." We noted other slips in a column headed "Clipperettes that Pass in the Night":

Although errors have been known to appear in Ye *Clipper*, some of the more picturesque items never see the light of play—we mean, day.

For example, in this week's issue we almost made Richard Sprague a "bun" instead of a "gun" collector. He is not interested in buns, however edible.

We came near mentioning that some residents live on "Sipyard" Lane. There is many a slip betwixt a sip and a ship, you see. The name, of course, was Shipyard Lane.

Also in time's nick, we changed Thomas W. Lawson the Eleventh to the Second. An economy of numbers.

Then there was that "panty" instead of "pantry" shower for the retired Sunday School superintendent.

In an editorial on the need for playgrounds, we wrote: "Duxbury needs more pubic (we meant public) facilities."

Came that first Christmas. After wishing all Duxbury residents a happy holiday, Snug Harbor Fish Market suggested that its customers "Order Your Oysters NOW!" Then came this gem:

"We will be open Christmas from eleven to noon to THUCK them for you." Fortunately, Carl Santheson, the burly proprietor, had a sense of humor. In another ad in which oysters were mentioned, the line "Closed Mondays" appeared when a reader asked when the oysters were open, we referred him to the shellfish constable. Another advertiser who mentioned "Medium Cleaned Shrimp" made his customers wonder why the shrimp were not cleaned more thoroughly.

Duxbury residents travel a great deal, and add to readership interest by mailing in post cards from remote places, and families who are leaving will frequently subscribe to the *Clipper* to keep abreast of local affairs. When one family moved, we received a photograph. In the cut line we reported:

Mr. and Mrs. John X, formerly of Washington Street, are shown in Cairo, Egypt, mounted on Egyptian jeeps, better known as camels. They visited the pyramids, mosques and a bazaar, and then, in a mood nostalgic, had luncheon in an American restaurant. Left to right in the photo are Mrs. X, her daughter, Carol; son, John; daughter, Susan, held in place by her father. The X family are all wearing fezzes. One guide is wearing a turban, the other a skull cap picked up in a bazaar-bargain basement. The X family will live in Sumatra, Indonesia, for two years.

Mr. X, whom we had never met, was not even in the photo. We mistook the Arab guide for him! In a later issue we apologized:

John X is a tall, handsome gentleman who, with his family, is now in Indonesia. In a recent issue we mistook a good-looking squat Arab guide, wearing a fez, for him. Nothing fezzed, he sent us this cablegram from Sumatra: "NOT I SAID THE SPARAB." This is the best sparable we have heard in ten Sundays.

Most *Clipper* readers greeted our miscues with amused tolerance. One note:

I have had my fourth *Clipper* in the hospital. When I read in the last issue that I was home feeling fine after a few days here— well, shall we call it the tall story of the year or blame it on too much New Year's celebration? Three and a half weeks are a long time.

Another slip led to this notice in "Around Town:"

When Crary Trimble read in the *Clipper* that she had accompanied her husband to New York City she took the next train down to keep us honest.

The first serious error occurred in the "Who Is It?" feature in midsummer of 1950. Mr. X, we reported, married a charming Radcliffe graduate in 1931. After a few more biographical clues, we added: "His first-born arrived in 1930." (instead of the correct 1932). Mr. X did not sue.

Readers were also puzzled when a garden contractor advertised for a "part of full-time adult woman." The "of" should have been "or."

This note came from the Caribe Hilton, San Juan, Puerto Rico:

It's too bad we had to leave town so hurriedly, but I'm sure you'll agree that there wasn't much choice. When your story in the *Clipper* hit the newsstands about my bagging seven geese at Silver Lake, as against the legal limit of two, it was simply a question of getting to the airport without delay. Actually, I shot only one, but who expects the warden to believe that? There was the whole grim account in black and white in the *Clipper*. Fortunately, I can report the situation could have been worse. The people here in the Caribbean have offered me sanctuary until it is safe to return.

Clipper headlines were as informal as the social notes or news stories. In a November, 1950, issue the lead story was headed:

SURVEY SHOWS 28 PER CENT OF SCHOOL CHILDREN HAVE ANEMIA

Another story on the front page gave election results in the state election. I was horrified when, while proofreading, I came upon this arresting headline:

DUXBURY S – – – S ON FLAT RATE PROPOSAL

One of the linotypers had playfully substituted this stark statement for the head:

FLAT RATES REJECTED
BY DUXBURY VOTERS

My version appeared in the *Clipper*, of course, but the boys in the shop printed half a dozen "souvenir" copies as a gag.

On paper-folding night, Debbie and George came over. When the *Clippers* arrived at seven o'clock I put two bundles on either end of the long dining-room table. Just before Debbie and George started folding, I put a souvenir copy on top of each pile and left the room. Suddenly Debbie, who always scanned the news before starting to fold, shrieked. "My God, look at the headline in the second column." Bobbie, who knew nothing of the gag, turned pale when she saw the paper.

"This whole form will have to be printed over," she said, "even if it means the *Clipper* will be delayed. Call Tom Porter right this minute."

While I held the receiver down and pretended to blast Tom, they sat down for a drink, figuring there would be no folding. They were relieved when I finally said it was just a hoax, that only six phony copies had been printed, and I had four.

"Burn them before anyone else sees them or we'll be out of business," Bobbie said. I did just that.

Thursday afternoon an Island Creek resident called.

"Something terrible has happened," he said. "I suppose you know all about it by now."

I was sure, from his excitement, that somebody had been murdered. "What is it?"

"Look, are you kidding? 'What is it?' I thought you said *The Duxbury Clipper* was going to be a nice friendly little paper for all the family. You print a thing like that on the front page and ask what happened? You mean to say you aren't even worried?"

"Look, Fred. It was the school doctor, not I, who said all those children had anemia. I knew it would hit some parents hard, but we report news as it happens, not the way people would like to have it happen. A weekly paper is a mirror that—"

"News as it happens—bunk," Fred said. "You should know by now that this is Duxbury, not Skid Row. I'll tell you another thing. It's against postal regulations to send that kind of filth through the mail. I'm glad I got the *Clipper* this morning before my kids had a chance to see that disgusting headline on the front page."

I was speechless. Not for a moment had it occurred to me that Fred received a copy of the "souvenir" edition. Only Bobbie and I could leave copies of the *Clipper* at the post office (unless we gave others approval). Somehow—and it remains a mystery to this day—one "shocker" got mixed up with the regular copies. When I explained the gag—a gag all at once humorless—to Fred, he was disappointed.

"In that case," he said, "maybe I better keep my rare copy. Someday it may be a collector's item."

*Some*day? It already was.

By that first midsummer *The Duxbury Clipper* was churning through choppy seas. Although Bobbie and I were making a modest profit, we lagged behind the weekly publishing costs with cash-in-hand despite the money I was earning on the side. The work load was still heavy towards the end of July when I locked myself for four days into Cid Ricketts Sumner's studio, a converted water tower on Surplus Street, and concentrated on the adventure book for seven hours a day. Cid's telephone was disconnected while she was in Scotland, and there were no other interruptions.

Having no time for a spit-and-polish job, I took a wild flyer. Instead of writing a preliminary draft of the remain-

94

ing chapters of *Tom Stetson and the Blue Devil*—some fifty thousand words—and making the usually necessary revisions later, I turned out the original and two carbons, completing the book two days before the deadline. After proofing the manuscript, I retyped one page, sent off my beautiful prose, hoping the beauty would be in the eye of the beholder, and waited for an indignant letter from the publisher. To our delighted surprise, the editor sent a check for five hundred dollars a few days later with a note that included this comment: "We think this book is the best of the series." The moral seems to be: Take it easy, chum, and don't reach, and all will be champagne and skittles.

Although a thousand-dollar advance is scarcely a munificent payment for a "juvenile," Bobbie and I thought it quite acceptable for less than thirty-five hours of actual work. And that second payment of five hundred dollars came just in time to keep the *Clipper* afloat, as did another check for five hundred dollars we received later from the *Ford Times* for writing two brief articles—one on the Peabody Museum in Cambridge, the other on the first Pilgrim fort in Plymouth.

The *Clipper* did not have smooth sailing for long, for our printing and mailing costs increased to approximately two hundred and fifty dollars a week when we put out ten-page papers. The lack of capital was beginning to hurt as our accounts receivable built up. By Christmas of 1950 we were flat broke, although we had several hundred dollars tied up in accounts receivable. This posed somewhat of a problem, for we had invited Auntie May, Bobbie's grandaunt, to spend the holiday with us. Auntie May had thoughtfully provided a huge turkey; but what about all the fixin's? Whether it was poor management on my part mattered not. The grim truth was that there was insufficient cash on hand for groceries!

Bobbie was nothing daunted. "No problem at all," she said.

"There is that extra warming pan up there in the attic, and a few other disposable antiques." We sold the warming pan and a few other items to an antique dealer for twenty dollars and enjoyed a festive Christmas dinner.

If Auntie May had known all the circumstances, she would have been horrified.

CHAPTER 11

"Rural life is hard, and the publisher of a rural weekly
must share the hardships of his readers. You may find
that in a poor season, you'll be paid off in potatoes for
subscriptions."

—THE GOVERNMENT BROCHURE

There are newspaper authorities who say a country weekly is not run for profit. This generalization is ridiculous. It would not have seemed so ridiculous to Bobbie and me, however, as we moved into the final weeks of 1950.

By the end of the year, the *Clipper*, still pitching and rolling, had grossed about nine thousand dollars, and we netted about a third of that amount. A profit of three thousand dollars is a fair return for eight months' work on a new enterprise, true, but we knew that some of our advertisers were merely trying to help us get established. Kenneth and Ruth Wakefield ("two of the nicest persons I ever met," said the late Ernie Pyle), proprietors of the world-famed Toll House in Whitman (you simply must try Toll House Cookies some time), were Duxbury residents. When they ran Toll House ads in the *Clipper*, we felt that our little weekly was acquiring more prestige than it deserved.

Another friend and neighbor was the late Harry Chisholm, president of the Montgomery Frost Company of Boston. Mr. Chisholm ran several large ads in the paper even though, he explained, "my family think I'm crazy." Henry Pierce, former banking commissioner of Massachusetts, and now president of the Merchants Co-operative Bank in Boston, collared me at a meeting one night and asked why I had not solicited an ad from him. He has run ads in the *Clipper* ever since. This kind of advertising gave the *Clipper* tone, as did the small display ad which S. S. Pierce Company of Boston ran during the summer:

WE DELIVER TO CERTAIN
STREETS IN DUXBURY

Some of our early advertisers were deadbeats, we unhappily discovered. "Does Your Roof Leak?" one artisan asked before he leaked out of town, leaving behind a stream of unpaid bills, including the *Clipper*'s. Later another roof surgeon ran a series of ads and left town. These reverses came at just about the time Bobbie and I were gaining insight into human nature from the vantage point of a country editor. What was there about roof surgeons that induced them to run into debt and out of town? Even if both gentlemen had stuck around sticking their creditors, we could not have bartered with them, since our roof did not leak at the time.

What weekly editor has not at one time or another engaged in barter? Our first experience in this historic form of American enterprise came when a fish peddler (who no longer is in business) refused to pay our bills, even when we wrote on them "Please" and "Pay this damn thing or else," in that order. Finally we had to settle for fish twice a week. Later, when his ads got bigger, we switched to lobster.

"But I don't like lobster, Mummy," Meg said.

"Everyone," said Mummy, "should do at least two things a week which he dislikes. It is part of character training. In your case, you will eat lobster twice a week until you learn to like it. I hope, by that time, that Pete won't stop running ads."

One day Bobbie asked me to help a man carry in a used sofa. "It shows the power of *Clipper* classified ads," she said. "I ran the ad only one week and picked up a nice used sofa for twelve dollars."

"Look, darling," I said, "we can't even afford a used bottle of gin, so why in—"

"Shush," she said. "Let me explain. Sally X owes us almost seventy dollars for her upholstery ad, so it won't cost us a cent to get this new used sofa upholstered."

"What about the legs of this sofa?" I asked. "They are practically falling off."

"You forget that nice man in West Duxbury who is advertising his chair hospital. It won't cost us a cent to fix up this sofa. Later we'll put in a classified for a good second-hand wing chair."

"But why? Why? We already have enough wing chairs."

"We'll have some of that upholstering money left over, silly. It won't cost seventy dollars to do that sofa, I'm sure."

Barter has its place in grass-roots American economy, but this primitive example of laissez-faire policy has definite limitations. During the early years of the *Clipper*, we acquired, through bartering agreements forced upon us, a supply of tailor-made slip-covers, sneakers, lawnmowers, ice cream (we just couldn't eat all we were entitled to), ice buckets and foundation garments. We no longer exchange *Clipper* space for such gracious accessories to modern living, but in those upswing days we were too naive to realize that once word got around that a plumber had fixed our dripping faucet in exchange for a little ad, a baker, carpenter or electrician might keep deferring payment on his advertising bills until we were forced to "take it out in trade." There were enough normal businessmen around, however, to restore our faith in the eventual success of the *Clipper*. We were especially glad that an advertising-minded funeral director was one of them.

There were honest advertisers, we knew, who were too strapped to pay. In a nearby town was an attractive restaurant we'll call the Norwegian Blue Barn. When the owner was unable to pay the *Clipper* bill, we asked Herman Smith, our distinguished "food editor," to mention the succulent morsels served at Norwegian Blue Barn *smörgåsbord*. This plug helped, but with a big overhead, prospects were not bright. Would it help if we brought a group of friends over for dinner to liquidate the bill? we asked the proprietor. She was delighted. This arrangement lasted as long as the Norwegian Blue Barn.

When the manager of a shore-line nightclub kept ignoring our bills, the temptation was to turn over his account to a lawyer. If collected, this is profitable procedure—for the lawyer. We took a different course. One night we invited three couples to his place, which we shall call El Ranchito, since that is not its name. Everyone had cocktails, a gourmet dinner with appropriate wine for each course, and white green things or green white things with the coffee. When the waiter brought the check, I signed it and gave him the customary tip.

"Oh, I'm sure this will be all right," I said when he stood there, hesitant and uncertain. "And please be sure to tell the manager his Lobster Thermidor was most delicious, and his Chablis excellent. Tell him we enjoyed the dinner so much we can't wait to come back."

We accepted no more ads from El Ranchito, but the door is not closed. Even full-page ads will be acceptable—if paid for in advance.

After the *Clipper* had been sailing for a few months, Tom Porter asked us how we liked the life of a country editor.

"It's no end of fun," I said. For one thing, it was gratifying to discover that the *Clipper* had become a Duxbury institution. That, after all, was more important than any such bourgeois consideration as money.

"I want to tell you what a fine contribution to the community *The Duxbury Clipper* is," one old-time resident wrote in "Sounding Off." "It enlarges the common bonds of interest among us, gives a sense of general fellowship and good will and is edited with great tact. It is a fine example of the best in reportorial work."

A country editor's mail is full of quaint surprises. One day we received two letters from a subscriber who lived in a Boston suburb: "November 5, 12 o'clock noon. I did not receive the *Clipper* this week. Please send me one immediately." Second letter: "November 5, 2:30 P.M.: My *Clipper* just came, so don't bother to send me one."

Particularly pleasing were the brief exchanges we had with a widow in her eighties. Brisk and forthright, Mrs. X had an imperious manner worthy of a direct descendant of King

Caesar Ezra Weston. When a copy of the *Clipper* was late in arriving at her Brookline, Massachusetts, address, she wrote:

Gentlemen: Has the *Clipper* gone out of print? No paper this week. Kindly refer to the above address and don't neglect me again.

P.S. I prefer *The Duxbury Clipper* to *The Saturday Review of Literature* or *The Atlantic Monthly*.

We were still purring with pleasure a couple of weeks later when Mrs. X phoned us from Brookline: "Are you the young man responsible for putting out the *Clipper*?"

"Why, yes, and it's so nice of you to—"

"I received two copies of the *Clipper* this week. *One* is enough." Mrs. X had a curt manner that was heightened when she slammed a telephone receiver.

Her prize remark was made at an open hearing to discuss a proposed funeral parlor in Duxbury.

"I have been living in this town for eighty years," she said, waving a tightly wrapped black umbrella, "and have never felt the need for a funeral parlor, so why should we have one now?" There was some tittering, but nobody laughed. There was therefore no need for Mrs. X to bounce her umbrella off anyone's head. The petition, of course, was denied.

There was also the summer dowager with an accent as broad as it was long. Did she want *The Duxbury Clipper* mailed to her while she was in Florida?

"Heavens, *no!*" she said, hanging up before we could ask why.

Yes, it was no end of fun. . . .

It was no end of fun until someone who sounded like a punch-drunk prizefighter called from Boston one afternoon.

"Look, pal . . . Youse put out dat newspaper down dere?"

"Yes, indeed." Well, we thought, the *Clipper* was certainly getting around. Another subscriber, just think. . . .

"Well, pal, some of da boys might take a little ride down dere to talk to you, see? About dat take-a-buck routine, get it, pal?"

We remembered, after this smoothie had hung up. In a recent issue we had quoted a Boston politico to this effect: "Sure, I'll take a buck." He must have had a friend who had a friend in Duxbury. P.S. Da boys never bothered to come down.

Early in 1951 Tom Porter, in a cloak-and-dagger manner, again asked how we liked running the *Clipper*.

We told him our enthusiasm had not waned.

"Well, I was just wondering. I take it you wouldn't be interested in selling the paper?"

"Well, I don't know," I said, trying to match his arch manner. How flattering, I thought, to think that a business you pulled out of your hat could be sold for cash. The *Clipper* —merely an idea, after all, for it owned no office, plant or equipment—was an asset that was worth money. Not that we had any intention at the moment of selling the paper. Bobbie had mentioned more than once that she wanted to see what it would look like when it grew up.

"Has someone made an offer, Tom?" I thought of the memorable shipboard conversation J. Pierpont Morgan once had with Andrew Carnegie.

"You know, J.P.," Andy had said, "I should have asked you for a hundred million more when I sold you U.S. Steel."

"Well, you would have got it if you had," Morgan said.

Any deal in which *The Duxbury Clipper* might become involved would be on a somewhat smaller scale, of course, but the principle was the same. Think big, ask much, hold firm.

"Yep, the William Randolph Hearst of the South Shore

has made a definite offer." He was referring to the publisher of several South Shore weeklies.

"Of how much?"

"A thousand dollars," Tom said.

What a blow to our ego! "Look, Tom, a thousand dollars wouldn't buy a man a fancy coffin, and the *Clipper*—at least, as far as Bobbie and I are concerned—is a much nicer thing to have than the fanciest coffin."

"So you don't think much of the proposal?"

Just tell Mr. Clutchpenny to let us mull over his offer for a little while. Five or ten years, say."

Several months later a Harvard professor of English, whom we had met at a writers' conference, dropped in with his nephew. This handsome young man, who was on the staff of the *Wall Street Journal*, was interested in launching a weekly newspaper in a New England town about the size of Duxbury. How did one go about it?

"The first requisite," I said, "is to have a wife who says, 'Look, dear, instead of lazing around, why don't you start a little newspaper?' " I also warned him not to believe everything professors of journalism advised, since the bold move often pays off as far as a country weekly is concerned. A capable journalist with a fresh approach should not, moreover, worry if he does not measure up to the standards of that mythical "average weekly editor." Measure up or down? Having read several varying versions of the "average weekly editor," this is our composite. He is around middle age and round in the middle. He is apt to be male and belongs to at least one civic group and a press association. He handles job printing and is unfailingly sweet to his big advertisers. His favorite novel is *Peyton Place* and his advertising rates are much too low. He is a pessimist who is bogged down with expensive equipment that is always getting out of whack.

He fears competition from other media and is crushed by his work load.

When *The Duxbury Clipper* was launched, I was male, middle-aged and certainly would have read *Peyton Place* had it been published. I have never joined a civic group nor ever attended a press association meeting. We have no costly equipment to bog us down, and are never, accordingly, even tempted to accept job printing. But why go on? All the criteria that are mentioned in the same breath with the average weekly editor are so varied as to be meaningless. Just as towns differ, so will country editors vary, and their papers will reflect their temperaments and personalities.

Another day, two journalism students from Boston University asked how a country editor made his sheet popular with its readers. Our answer was that the aim of a good weekly is to be respected, not popular.

A country weekly should print news without fear of criticism and always, of course, within the bounds of good taste. The weekly whose editor is a mute captive of his advertisers insults its readers' intelligence, and if it lasts, the town can blame itself.

From time to time other prospective country editors have dropped in to hear something of the pitfalls and pratfalls that contribute to the placid existence of this gentle profession. One particularly able young man, whose wife is a former advertising executive, was a reporter and feature writer for a New York daily. If clever kids like these want to buy *The Duxbury Clipper*, Bobbie reasoned, it must be a good thing. "Let's make it better."

(P.S.: The reporter-feature writer today is a successful editor for a New York book publisher. Someday we may ask him if he still wants to buy the *Clipper*.)

"But not now," says Bobbie. "Suppose he says 'yes'?"

In 1957, Bobbie and I turned down another offer for the *Clipper*. The bid of $25,000 received a flat *no!* By October of 1959 we were running our first fourteen-page paper, and Bobbie, while pleased, was still curious.

"I still want to see what the *Clipper* will be like when it grows up," she said.

When Tom Porter told us early in December of 1950 that he would no longer be able to handle the *Clipper*, we looked around for a newspaper plant where we could job out our expanded weekly. Of several available, we narrowed the choice to two establishments, both of which published their own weeklies. One publisher offered to print the *Clipper* for $25 a week less than the other, and although his plant was farther from Duxbury, we were tempted to accept his bid. I left a copy of the most recent issue of the *Clipper* with this publisher and told him to set the masthead and "standing" ads unless he heard anything to the contrary within the following two days.

During this interval, we decided to switch to the Observer Press in South Braintree, a forty-minute drive from Duxbury. This union shop had highly skilled operators and fancy equipment, including a Ludlow machine used for making "heads," an innovation for us.

"We also have an Elrod for making column rules," Foreman John Riley remarked the first day he showed Bobbie and me around the cluttered establishment.

Had we known what an Elrod was, we might have inquired about column rules, or vice versa. Having not even the dimmest notion what either term meant, we kept mum, nodded sagaciously, and tried to look intelligent.

Meanwhile, Bobbie had called the other publisher to tell him of our decision, and his wife took the message. Mrs. Publisher, apparently, neglected to pass the word to her husband before he had set the *Clipper* copy, and he sued *The Dux-bury Clipper* for two hundred dollars. We lost sleep, won suit.

The first edition printed by the Observer Press ran a boxed notice on the front page:

NO MORE GLOSSY PAPER

Rising costs and the difficulty of obtaining glossy paper force us regretfully to shift with this week's issue to regular newsprint.

When and if conditions permit the use of machine-gloss, we shall be glad to do so. There are other changes in the format of the *Clipper*, all occasioned by necessity. We might add that this is the first issue that has not been hand-folded, a job we and the friends who helped week after week are happy to abandon. We hope that with its new coat of paint, the *Clipper* will remain seaworthy.

I was still naïve enough to think glossy paper was preferable to less expensive and more appropriate newsprint! Not, of course, that I made *all* the mistakes possible for a novice editor to make.

There simply wasn't time for that.

CHAPTER 12

"It is a courtesy to your guests to have their visits mentioned in this column. It is a courtesy to your friends, too, to let them know of your own visits and of other interesting events. Items for this column are always welcome, and the cooperation of those who contribute them is much appreciated."

—THE VINEYARD GAZETTE

By 1951, the *Clipper* had sloughed off, except for occasional lapses, such filler thrillers as the "Irish Mossers of Scituate," and was concentrating more on the local scene, with an all-out drive for "Around Town" items:

Did you just get an interesting letter from your son stationed at Fort Dix or in Japan? Is the engagement of your daughter about to be announced? Did Father shoot a hole in one or did Junior slug three home runs in a sandlot baseball game? Has anyone had roast opossum lately, and has any Marine been seen wearing a Truman campaign button? We want news from every part of Duxbury—West, North and North by Northwest. So let us know what you're adoin', will you *please?*

Earlier we had mentioned that the *Clipper* would "be delighted to publish any news of birthday parties, wedding anniversaries or neighborhood parties, shindigs or jamborees. Sometimes our crystal ball is clouded and we don't see all that happens. Won't you jot down names, places, and dates and send them in, *please?*"

Later the suggestion was more explicit:

If you have been on a trip, been rescued from an ice floe, won the Nobel Prize (or, better still, the Irish Sweepstakes), entertained bizarre guests, celebrated a birthday anniversary, caught a shark, moved, eloped, treed a wildcat, cut a new tooth (especially if you are over 21), sold out, had an operation, painted your house an unusual color, just been married, robbed or shot; have stolen anything, lost your hair or your temper, or have been bitten by a dog, horse or cow or nipped by a lobster, phone, drop a post card or wire *The Duxbury Clipper*.

A bit silly, of course, but productive of results. Our prize beat came when a local angler boated a 573-pound tuna. We ran a four-column cut with this story. Later the Boston *Daily Record* told its readers this was the biggest bluefin tuna boated in the Bay State during two years.

Despite mounting evidence that the *Clipper* was being happily recognized, we felt we were not running enough political or police news. Town officials do not always think the public has a right to know what is going on, and tend to keep their actions secret. Many public officials in small towns consider themselves a law unto themselves, believing that what they do is none of the taxpayers' business. According to the *Clipper*'s oldtimer (he was not referring to Duxbury politicians, natch), telling lies, as far as politicos are concerned, is not so much a vice as a manner of speaking.

"To git elected, Snoop-Scoop, polls kin only be half truthful. Some are less half than others, but none is more than half. They tell all the truth some of the time and none of the truth most of the time. Mostly they tell half truths, and the trouble is, son—"

"Yes?"

"Trouble is, people believe the wrong half."

Even discounting the oldtimer's cynicism, it is true of many communities that politicians operate in a hush-hush manner. As a result, rumors, distortions of truth and malicious lies are spread which would get nowhere if officials were forthright.

Public officials who try to conceal news are naive, for we have yet to learn of any news a newspaper wanted that it didn't get in one way or another. Often elected or appointed officials in small towns are conscientious and honest. All they need is a course in public relations.

The country editor's role? When he walks down to the post office, he enjoys seeing people standing around reading his paper, pleased that he is supplying a link that ties the community together: Carol Anne has just announced her engagement. . . . Bay Road is being repaved. . . . Sally has the lead in the high school play, and Billy won a PTA scholarship. Little things along with important items. While reporting the little things, the editor must think of his responsibility. . . .

Bobbie and I, unaware of any responsibility at first, were more concerned with the *Clipper's* reception. Accordingly, we were encouraged when we received dozens of flattering letters. "Each copy of the *Clipper* is like a visit home," a former resident wrote from Monrovia, California. "Such a wonderful thought—your decision to print a Duxbury newspaper!" We were further pleased when the Duxbury Free Library announced that it would keep a complete collection of bound *Clippers,* or when Duxbury residents who moved, wrote: "I can't imagine moving to a new house without having the *Clipper* coming every week." Summer residents, also, appended notes to subscription requests: "We are always reluctant to leave Josselyn Avenue, but thanks to your *Clipper,* we don't feel too far removed when the snow begins to fly." Many prospective residents asked that the paper be sent to them so they could become acquainted with the town: "My good friend, Joe Marto," wrote William P. Sawyer, president of the Watertown Federal Savings Bank, "has just informed me that just as everybody in Philadelphia reads the *Inquirer,* so does everyone in Duxbury read the *Clipper.* As a future resident of your town I have been advised to soak up as much local atmosphere as possible by reading the *Clipper,* and would appreciate your entering my name upon your subscription list and forward bill for the same."

How wonderfully reassuring, dum de dum. . . . And then another little jolt.

"I love *The Duxbury Clipper,*" an elderly woman told a friend, "but I do wish it wasn't quite so conservative."

We had always considered this elder stateswoman as unfailingly conservative as she was kindly and cultured. Something had to be done out of hand, and the more *tout de suite* the better. The first step, we decided, was to run more news from the Selectmen. The second, to carry more police news.

Although our relations with the Duxbury Selectmen had always been friendly, it was difficult at first to get the three gentlemen to ladle out news. We had no precedent to cite when one of them said, "After all, this town has gotten along pretty well for over three hundred years without having a newspaper meddling in its affairs." The inference was clear. We were meddlesome newcomers. Well, there were other newcomers, too, we thought, and some of them were just as tired as we were of hearing that weary old refrain: "Seems to me this town did all right for quite a spell without any interference from you newcomers. They always want to be reformers. But they'll learn, they'll learn. They always do...."

When a Selectman asked why he should give the *Clipper* any news, since none of his predecessors had ever been subjected to such indignity, we told him no coercion was involved. "But the *Clipper* will run a blank column each week headed 'Selectmen News,'" we told the gentleman. That strategy, alas, was never necessary, for "Selectmen News" has since been a regular feature of the *Clipper*.

It was an uphill battle to get permission to read the police blotter. "We aren't even allowed to read the blotter ourselves," the Selectmen told us.

Police Chief James T. O'Neil, who retired in 1959, was the first chief the Duxbury Police Department ever had, and for a few years, was the entire police force. Chief O'Neil, whom we have always admired because of his tact, compassion and bed-rock common sense, is a person who can charm a bird down from a tree if the spirit moves him, but he can also be stubborn on occasion. He flatly refused to let me read the blotter, and was backed up by the Selectmen.

We countered with a little playful strategy, counting on a certain juxtaposition of letters to the editor to strengthen our position. In one issue, "Sounding Off" contained these communications:

Aside from the useful role of *The Duxbury Clipper* in its advertising department, compact shape, fine printing and distinguished name, not to mention its many articles of interest and value, I feel it has made "One Town" of our local "world." It brings news from all parts of town, which is of special interest to those who are no longer active in town affairs. It makes the readers acquainted with many useful and talented persons and broadens their horizons. So I extend my thanks and appreciation to the editors and congratulate them on their enterprise, initiative, and well deserved success.

This letter was written and signed by a highly respected member of the community.

Under it we published another note from another solid citizen and a member of a distinguished family:

The enclosed clippings are from *The Townsman*, Wellesley's weekly newspaper. Each week one or two columns are given over to police notes, thus keeping the town in touch with this department. May I suggest it might be an added attraction to the *Clipper?*

"Very interesting," said Chief O'Neil, grinning. "*Very* interesting. But this is Duxbury, not Wellesley."

The following issue of the *Clipper* contained letters signed "Bored Reader" and "Disgruntled," both written by the *Clipper* editor:

Dear Editor. Your paper is useful. The size and shape makes it perfect lining for blueberry baskets.

In the second epistle we moved closer to the target:

I understand from reading *The Duxbury Clipper* that there are never any fires in Duxbury, that the police blotter is a complete blank, and that no news from the Selectmen must be good news. Doesn't anything ever happen beside fairs and auctions? Cranberries a lead story!!! Why don't you smarten up? I'm burned because you give the paper away. Damn it, I can't even cancel my subscription.

Incidentally, there would be no reader interest in a weekly if all subscribers were completely uncritical. When either a brick or a bouquet is tossed at an editor, he is flattered, for

113

he knows his product is being read. We publish "Dear Sir You Cur" letters, if they are signed—although we will withhold names on request. In appended parentheses we may make some such snide comment as: "Our handwriting expert scolded us for calling the writer of this letter a moron. 'After a careful scrutiny,' he said, 'I concluded that this person is merely a dim-wit, not a moron of the classic pattern.' "

After publishing the letters signed "Bored Reader" and "Disgruntled" we received letters from loyal readers rebuking the authors of those "anonymous" letters: "We were quite disturbed by the comments in last week's edition concerning the *Clipper*," a housewife wrote. "We feel very fortunate in having such a nice paper and enjoy it no end."

Readers are less critical if you poke fun at yourself, dear editor. One subscriber wanted to know what the *Clipper*'s editorial policy was, sarcastically adding, "I am told that the policy of your poltroon of a political editor is 'that of sensible editors.' What in hell is that?"

"Sensible editors never say," we answered.

Long before we launched a weekly, we learned that it is silly to argue with women, the clergy or the press. Although we don't always return fire, it's fun on occasion to return quip for quip.

"Would you kindly send me the proper form so that I can subscribe to your paper for my son who is spending the next year in Alaska and wants to keep track of what happens in the United States?" one reader asked. We advised that "for complete coverage of what happens in the U.S., we suggest *The New York Times* and John Foster Dulles' diary as supplementary reading to the *Clipper*."

Chief O'Neil, despite all this editorial barrage, held firm. Then came another plant by the snide editor, complaining that the *Clipper* "wasn't political enough." Here it is: "I have heard that your paper is biased and colored. I rose to your defense immediately. I said it was colorless." Finally, this last phony communication: "Your paper is as flat as a pancake. Don't you know what's going on in this town?"

Once more, gallant readers rose to the defense of the *Clipper*.

Finally we convinced Chief O'Neil of our right to read the police blotter, and agreed to run a regular column headed "Police Diary," which would contain items of community interest without damaging reputations. Here are sample entries from the "Police Diary:"

October 18: 7 A.M. Police receive complaint that three horses are running around Tinkertown. A field driver was summoned to round up the horses.

9:10 A.M. Woman reports losing a pair of black leather pumps at Hall's Corner.

3:45 P.M. Police notified that 35 panes of glass were broken in building on cranberry bog. A small-gauge shotgun and a 22 rifle were used. Four juveniles who admitted the offense were turned over to custody of probation officer.

October 19: 4:10 P.M. Plymouth police warn Duxbury police to be on watch for counterfeit ten-dollar bills. The bills are slightly off color, but good specimens. Duxbury police warn local merchants to be on guard.

7:30 P.M. Police to scene of family argument.

11:55 P.M. Police called to quell another family argument.

October 20: 8:30 P.M. Police called to scene of neighborhood argument.

November 5: 2:05 P.M. Horse reported on loose. Field driver summoned.

2:35 P.M. Recover stolen duck decoys.

8:35 P.M. Complaint from West Street resident about four heifers in yard. Police tell owners to remove them.

November 30: 1:10 P.M. Call from State Police reports man Duxbury holds warrant for picked up in Wells, Maine.

4:40 P.M. Resident in with cat to be destroyed.

4:45 P.M. Resident complains cow loose on premises.

5:35 P.M. Resident calls to say her French poodle is missing.

11:35 P.M. Police summoned to Huckleberry Lane to investigate prowler.

December 4: 6:15 P.M. Police called to Huckleberry Lane to investigate Peeping Tom after resident fires shotgun blast at prowler.

December 10: 8:16 P.M. Peeping Tom reported shot at twice by Huckleberry Lane husband, whose wife has been annoyed by the prowler. The Peeping Tom got away unhurt.

After a few months, the *Clipper* dropped the "Police Diary," since many of its entries were trivial and repetitious. Chief O'Neil also felt that it tended to ridicule "Duxbury's finest" by its frequent allusions to chasing stray cows and horses and putting superannuated cats to sleep.

"What the people don't know," said Chief O'Neil, "is that we have to chase stray husbands as well as stray cows."

Now, if circumstances permitted mentioning these errant husbands, and *what* family disputes the police settled, along with the hazards connected therewith, the police would have gained the sympathy of most citizens! If any police blotter divulged all its secrets, including the booking of prominent citizens and the vagaries of certain housewives, it would have sent some residents packing. It bothered us after a while to know that Mrs. A was carrying on with Mr. B in a sequestered motel, their tawdry tryst unknown to their families. The blotter, not I, was a more appropriate repository for a wide range of foibles and escapades which are, beyond any peradventure of doubt, common in all small towns. After all, doesn't everything happen in the microcosm of almost any

116

community? What has Peyton Place that any New England community has not? Correct—a Grace Metalious. Anyone who thinks the police blotter in Peyton Place has a special aura all its own might be surprised to discover that it differs only in degree from the blotter in the next town down by the junction, for in every concentrated cluster of homo sap the spangled parade of life passes in review.

There was enough wholesome police news—stirring police news—to report in Duxbury, after all. We can recall two instances in which Officer Frank White of the night shift saved lives, and other examples of quick thinking and heroic measures taken in emergencies by other members of the force, including Tom Johnson, Larry Doyle, Bob Byrne, Frank Phillips, and his late father, Elmer Phillips.

Should a country newspaper, dredging up bilge, print ALL the news? Yea, say some editors. "I have always felt that whatever the Divine Providence permitted to occur I was not too proud to report," said Charles A. Dana. Really, now! In a small town the editor is not motivated by any consideration of pride, but rather of common sense. The argument that newspapers should print all news goes like this:

Newspapers don't make news. News makes newspapers. Those who criticize papers for publishing certain news would not think of blaming a mirror for the view it reflects, knowing very well that the mirror has no power within itself to reflect other than what is before it.

True. Also misleading. An editor, unlike a mirror, has a choice. He does have the power to choose and channel news, both good and bad. When there is significant news, we report it, but the *Clipper* refuses to print items that are more sensational than informative. If Papa dips too deeply into the punch bowl and winds up in the pokey, it would embarrass his family no end if the story popped out in print. His children

117

might be unmercifully ribbed by schoolmates. Derelictions on the part of public officials are another matter. They should be reported, but common sense should dictate the handling of personal scandals. A country weekly should report news accurately, but much more than its city counterpart, should respect personal rights of privacy, even if it sacrifices the spice of vice reporting. A weekly must reflect the town it serves and be consonant with its spirit and character.

What newspaper reports *all* the news? The *Globe* and *Herald* in Boston, like those in other metropolitan areas, sift news, observing the canons of good taste. They certainly would not publish some of the items that find favor with the readers of the *Mid-Town Journal*, a Boston weekly.

"My aim," said General Charles H. Taylor, founder of the Boston *Globe*, "has been to make the *Globe* a cheerful, attractive and useful newspaper that would enter the home as a kindly, helpful friend of the family. My temperament has always led me to dwell on the virtues of men and institutions rather than upon their faults and limitations. My disposition has always been to build up rather than to join in tearing down. My ideal for the *Globe* has always been that it should help men, women and children to get some of the sunshine of life, to be a little better and happier because of the *Globe*."

That is a good cornerstone for any country weekly newspaper.

Occasionally a story is so amusing an editor cannot resist using it, but if this means making a fool of a decent citizen, why can't a friendly paper print the story and omit names? Here's an example:

A popular Duxbury resident, wearing overalls, drove his wife to a railroad station (Route 128) where she boarded a train

118

for New York City. While he was putting her valise up on the rack, the train lurched into motion, and as he rushed down the aisle he ran into a woman. Being half an axe handle abaft the beam, he tried to edge by her sidewise, and in the process a button on his overalls caught the woman's purse.

"Help!" she shrilled. "Stop that thief! He stole my pocketbook!"

Mr. X, who did indeed give the impression that he was in a mad rush to leave the premises, was tripped in the ensuing commotion, and was harassed by some of the male passengers and the conductor until he explained what had happened. By this time he was on the way to Providence, Rhode Island, where he had to wait for an hour before boarding a homebound train. At his own station, another surprise awaited him.

His car had a ticket for exceeding the parking limit.

Although there is no need for the average weekly to "scoop" metropolitan papers that may have circulation in its area, this often happens. A country editor may receive a frantic call from a teenager who has just found a body washed onto the beach, or he may learn that a well-known resident has just used a plastic bag to commit suicide. In one instance, the *Clipper* gave casual mention to an item that would have rated more space in some of the Boston dailies. "Around Town" noted:

Mr. and Mrs. Walter Prince of Washington Street over the holidays entertained family members who are scattered over the world. Mrs. Prince's brother, Robert H. K. Marett, C.M.B., O.B.E., who is in the British diplomatic service, was here with his wife, daughter, and German governess. Mr. Marett is the new British Consul General in Boston. . . .

Shortly thereafter a guest at a cocktail party rebuked me for spreading such a false rumor.

119

"Why, only last Tuesday night," she said, "my husband and I had dinner with the British Consul in Boston, and he said nothing about leaving.... You should check official sources before printing such rubbish."

She almost had me convinced, since no Boston newspaper had mentioned any change in the Consul General's office. Our confidence in the efficiency of our pipeline was restored ten days later when radio and press confirmed the appointment of the new Consul General.

At another cocktail party, a guest sounded off about the panty-waisted *Clipper* which refused to print scandalous news. On the way home, he was arrested for driving under the influence and driving so as to endanger. The next time I met him, I couldn't resist teasing him.

"That was an interesting item, I know. Please accept my apology for not printing it."

Criticism? It's wonderful. In one week, we heard one person say the *Clipper* was too conservative and another remark: "Your paper is getting too sensational."

In the face of such criticism we invariably find solace in the words of an anonymous philosopher who said: "Those who mind don't matter, and those who matter don't mind."

In our anniversary issue, we looked back on some of the rocks and shoals that had imperiled our fragile craft during her first crossing:

"The toughest copy to write was accounts of weddings," I said. "You know, the bride wore a flock of talisman roses caught up to some heirloom beige Chantilly lace over a wine-dreg's red Belfast linen satin ivory bombazine and her attendants carried a bouquet of wintergreen-flavored Mexican jumping beans mixed with something that looked like endive. We still have trouble with this sort of things, girls, so if you must get hitched, please wear something simple like a tailored winding sheet or a long-sleeved pinafore."

The Duxbury Clipper observed its first birthday anniversary on May 10, 1951. Mr. and Mrs. William J. Powell of Washington Street sent two dozen red gladioli in honor of the happy occasion, and Mr. and Mrs. Robert Estabrook of Powder Point surprised us with a one-candled cake inscribed "Happy Birthday, Dear Clipper." Gail, four, blew out the candle on her first try, while Meg, Dave and Robert sang the birthday greeting. The card that came with the cake read: "Just a little birthday hello, with wishes for gladness that will grow and grow—in circulation."

By this time the *Clipper* was catching on. Bobbie and I were on lawn patrol duty at a church fair during the summer of 1951 when we noticed among items for sale at a silent auction an attractive wastebasket covered with historical items from *The Duxbury Clipper*. It not only sold in a hurry for eleven dollars, but Mrs. Robert Seymour, who donated it to the fair, received fourteen additional orders for *Clipper* wastebaskets. It was comforting to learn that *Clippers* were being put on wastebaskets rather than in them. Since then, Mrs. Seymour has sold well over a hundred of these useful souvenirs. One person may order a basket with racing news, while another wants one with paste-ups of fishing exploits. Some residents have received enough publicity to cover an entire container with news of their activities, and if a few more items are needed, it is simple to add some such item as: "John Doe, while viewing the foliage in Vermont and New Hampshire over the weekend, stopped in at Hanover to visit a former professor at Dartmouth College." If more copy is required, merely add: "John, who majored in European history while attending Dan Webster's alma mater, formerly known

121

as 'a refined lumber camp,' said the old place hasn't changed much. As Dan Webster used to say, 'It's a small college, but there are those who love it.' "

P.S. No, we receive no commission on the sales of *Clipper* wastebaskets.

CHAPTER 13

"There are very few holidays in the newspaper business—indeed, it is usually on holidays when the weekly editor works hardest—and the publisher has a much harder time getting a vacation than if he worked for someone else."

—THE GOVERNMENT BROCHURE

One of the principal appeals to the average newspaperman in publishing his own sheet is his wish for complete independence. He will soon discover, however, that he will have less independence at the start than if he were a reporter on a large daily, with the prestige of its circulation and money to back him up. There will be a great deal of drudgery at the outset, but the overall picture can be much brighter than the prophets of despair would have you think.

When weekly editors convene, they discuss such cheery

topics as rising production costs, inadequate labor force, reduced advertising lineage, archaic machinery and the dreadful competition from dailies, radio and television. This is one reason we don't attend their conventions.

A dozen weeklies have published this classic lament:

Running a newspaper is a snap, in case you haven't suspected it. Machinery does all the work. You sit in the office and write beautiful prose, and the machinery never breaks down or causes any trouble. Everybody brings in news and sport copy on time, and it is all carefully written and there are no mistakes in dates.

With hundreds of names and dates and places and circumstances in a single issue, nobody in the place ever gets anything wrong, even when working under pressure to meet the week's deadlines. Nothing ever gets left out of the paper by accident. Proofreaders are mind readers and can always know what was intended, whether he wrote it that way or not. You can always get the paper and other supplies when you need them.

You never get a vacation because you never need one. You never get tired. You spend long evenings at home loafing, and you have time to attend all public gatherings, board meetings, entertainment and social affairs. People never ask you to keep news out of the paper or to put tripe into it. If on very rare occasions a mistake does get into the paper, people who call about it always laugh understandingly and say, "That's perfectly all right."

Newspapering is a snap any way you look at it, and it's time the editors tell the public how wonderfully simple and easy it is.

And with that, we'll take our tongues out of cheeks, uncross our fingers, roll up our sleeves and start to work to get the paper out.

If weekly newspapering is such an exacting chore, what is its lure? Professor John H. Casey of the University of Oklahoma, an authority on journalism and advertising, suggests an answer:

Without its newspaper, the small-town American community would be like a school without a teacher or a church without a pastor. In the aggregate, the country newspaper determines the outcome of more elections, exerts a greater influence for constructive community progress, is read longer by more members of the family and constitutes with its millions of circulation and quadrupled millions of readers, a better advertising medium than any other group of newspapers or periodical publications.

When properly conducted, it cultivates so intensively its home news field that city dailies, farm journals and general magazines circulating in the same territory become only secondary influences.

Through service to its community, the country newspaper will not merely survive; it will continue to flourish as the most representative, most distinctive, most wholesome type of journalism America has ever produced.

A prospective weekly publisher can eliminate many headaches by selecting a growing community and jobbing his paper out to a print shop. (If the area you select is ready for a weekly, it won't be too far from a printer who will welcome your business, since it carries him "over the valleys.") You will discover, moreover, that you will get more work done in less time if your office (ours is in our hat) is not too conveniently located. We take issue with the government brochure when it says:

For you, a central location on a main street will be of value principally as a matter of prestige. So long as your plant is readily accessible to patrons who will visit you to pay their bills, purchase back copies, bring in news items, or just drop in to chat, its location is relatively unimportant. Since your product reaches the consumer through the mails or by newsstand sales, you do not have to place your plant at a main intersection. However, don't locate your plant where it would be inaccessible to the public, or in a run-down or disreputable neighborhood which your patrons would hesitate to enter.

Our advice is simple: The more inaccessible your business office is, the less you will be bothered by bores, village gossips and lonely hearts who merely seek a compassionate ear. Most folks with news prefer to mail it in, and any last minute items can be dropped on your front hall table while you are reading a good book or watching "Meet the Press" on TV. You bill your clients monthly, so there is no need for them to drop by to make a payment. Since you deliver your paper free by mail, everyone has a copy. Extra copies of the *Clipper* are available (for ten cents) at three conveniently located stores in Duxbury. Back copies? In ten years of *Clipper*ing, only rarely have we been asked for a back number.

The machinery that turns out the *Clipper* has often broken down, but only once—during the 1954 hurricane when electric failure forced us to come out a day late—has it missed its Thursday morning mailing deadline.

Let correspondents who bring in copy late fume if it is left out. Carefully written? What right has a weekly editor, who receives news from scores of organizations, to expect copy to be clean, limpid, sprightly and velvety smooth? We edit all copy, deleting and tightening where necessary, to make it conform to *Clipper* style. Out come such barbarisms as "he ejaculated" or "she asseverated" or "they expostulated" (country correspondents who show these symptoms of literary growing pains belong to the " 'Oh ho!,' he whinnied" school). It's the editor's job to give his paper a uniform, individual flavor.

Mistakes in dates can be serious, true. Years ago we put out a special two-page edition on Saturday because the charming young lady who wrote up the story of a church fair used the wrong date in the regular Thursday issue, and since this mistake might have jeopardized the success of the fair (which netted over three thousand dollars) we rushed a special issue into print, collecting enough revenue (advertising) to pay for it.

True, it is a pity, that with so many names and details in each issue, mistakes are bound to creep in against the pressure of inexorable deadlines. But why worry? Big dailies, since they have more opportunities to err than you (unless they are as closely proofread as *The Christian Science Monitor*), will out-classic you in the "picturesque" speech department. We found this gem in a leading Boston newspaper: "At eleven, in short pants, Norbert Wiener entered college. Before the age when most boys shave, he was a doctor scolastic societies sniff of philosophy."

Now, *there* is a lad who couldn't help becoming a mature genius.

The *Clipper*, in the long stretch, has run features on its miscues, and the resulting reading coefficient of interest has been surprisingly high. Having discovered that these confessionals were favorably received, we wrote late in 1951:

It won't be long, now, before we do a magazine piece titled "The Weekly and I." Betty MacDonald thought she had HER troubles, hey?

In recent weeks, the linotype operators and the *Clipper* editor, working as a perfect team, have had a "gitchen" remodeled, making some of our readers wonder whether we were in the rehabilitation-of-junior-delinquents business. We had a Duxbury gal in Heidelberg attending General Handy's "stiff" instead of "staff" meetings and mentioned that a local plumber was selling "team soilers" instead of "steam boilers." A prize boner appeared in an account of a wedding when Mary X, scheduled to be sister Jane's bridesmaid, was unable to reach Duxbury in time. Mrs. X, Jane's mother, served as matron of honor. Our account disrupted the X genealogy: "Mrs. X, sister of the bride, was matron of honor." Further along we described in sartorial detail what the missing Mary wore, and then, to heap horrors on horror's head, we had the mother of the bride wearing "slime" instead of "lime" chiffon. Of course we men are apt to get our flavors mixed up, girls, but in this case we were a bit more careless than usual.

Then we let the secret out:

You guessed it. We wrote the account of the wedding BEFORE it happened, and the switch balled us up. We understand there are still a few unmarried Katrinkas around, and herewith serve warning that if there is a substitute at the last minute for the groom, we may pull another boner.

In the account of another wedding, I wrote that the bride wore "floor-length lace mitts," which would indeed have been a feat.

When residents objected to the silt pumped from the bay into their back yards, the *Clipper* gaily assured them that lush greenery would cover the eyesore in a year or two. Nature, however, conspired to make a liar of the *Clipper*, for even several years later, unless you count a tuft of weed here, and a bit of crab grass there, the tundra remains—bleak, barren, desolate and uncharitably ungreen.

Last week's *Clipper* was a gem [we noted in another edition]. We left out a couple of ads, had the bookworm turning in the wrong direction, substituted the word "marital" for "martial" (not that there is always a great difference), forgot to identify Mystery House No. 13 (in a contest we were running), left the guide line instead of the normal head for West Duxbury Methodist Church (it came out "meth church...."), had the bridesmaids wearing the same dresses as the bride (must be the Mormon influence) and ... but why go on? Isn't it nice the Christmas holidays come only once this year?

One reader phoned to blast me for printing there would be a talk at the garden club on "Joy of Conversation."

"Why," she said, "when I got there I discovered the talk was on *conservation!* And tell me, Mr. Cutler, what joy is there in *that?*"

Often an innocent item may incense a reader. "Those who think Duxbury is strictly a Republican town," I wrote in one edition, "will be surprised to learn that Harry Truman got two votes for the board of public welfare in Duxbury."

Harrumph! A gentleman who knows his way around the journalistic pasture sounded off:

One does expect a Duxbury newspaper to be Republican, since it would not be popular otherwise, but surely your readers are entitled to objective reporting. The informality of the *Clipper* copy which is welcomed by most of us can easily include a few candid remarks without going quite so far as to be unconcernedly blatant.

In an editorial note we wrote: "Valid criticism, sir. We stand rebuked."

As for the errors, we commented:

We do not have time to look under every leaf or turn over every pebble in our relentless quest for truth. Sometimes we have to ask for information, since, for example, there have been a few four-year-old girls who haven't been asking us to their birthday anniversary parties in recent years. We also take this happy occasion to bring our statistics up to date. According to our most recent survey, there are now 10,385 weekly editors in Duxbury. We can't tell you who the last one is. The realtor who sold him a house wants us to wait until papers are passed.

Now and then something is accidentally left out of the paper. This fact explained the mystery of one glare. The young matron handling publicity for a local church gave us a look at a social that would have withered a cactus plant. During the spring thaw we discovered the reason. While raking the front lawn I found the typescript of the church news sent in months before that contained a notice of a covered-dish supper, with the cheerful punch line: "COME and see all the FRIENDS you didn't dream you had!"

During the early years of the *Clipper*, some of those handling publicity for churches gave us a bad time, complaining that other churches received more publicity than theirs. "Perhaps," I ventured, "the other churches have better publicity chairmen." This is one way to win enemies and make no good impression on people.

Do some readers insist on your publishing tripe? Yea. Equally insistent, we tell them to jump into a lake. It's all part of the game of chills, thrills and spills known to the editor of every country weekly. There was that sub-zero telephone conversation we had with Mrs. Outraged Mother, a pleasant variation of the Mrs. Josephine Dithers type.

"Did you not receive some poetry from my daughter Steffie?" she opened stiffly.

We had indeed. The kind that gives the word doggerel a bad name.

"Sorry, Mrs. X, but your daughter's delightful poem didn't quite fit our editorial needs at this time, because of other commitments and..." This kind of editorialese, which we had been taught for years by masters of verbal sleight-of-hand who admit, "We know what we want, but we don't know what it is," would surely placate this disturbed parent, we thought.

"Editorial needs, hogwash," she said, off on the mother-cub gambit. "You publish poems all right. I've seen poems by Alison Arnold and Cid Ricketts Sumner that wasn't half so good as Stephanie's 'Ode to a Horseshoe Crab.'" A note of tenderness crept into her soprano. "Steffie stayed up half the night writing that poem."

"I know, but—"

"Two weeks ago you had a poem about a two-car garage. It seems to me that folks in Duxbury are just as interested in horseshoe crabs."

I tried to think while she ranted. A poem about a two-car

garage? Of course. Mrs. X was referring to a quatrain that took a snide dig at the opponents of a proposed new school:

> Oh, deliver the town from the misinformed citizen
> Who spews forth an inaccurate barrage.
> His only concern is his tightly clutched purse,
> Yet he sports two cars in his garage.

"Well," I said lamely, "that poem was timely, and—"

"Shut up," she said. "I've heard enough. I just want you to know that all our neighbors who read Steffie's poem think it's grand, just grand. We could have sent it to the Cousin Susan editor of the other paper we get, but I thought it only decent to let the *Clipper* print it first. Just send it back."

Well, sending it back was a lot better than having to read it back over the telephone.

"You never get a vacation because you never can get away from the grind," complain the unhappy brotherhood of country editors. Nonsense. Almost any week after the first two years of operation, Bobbie and I could take five days off a week without interrupting the voyages of the *Clipper*. We have even taken a six-day vacation, and we now have the situation well enough in hand to go off for longer stretches if we wish. This is in abrupt contrast to the early days of the *Clipper* when we mentioned one of our jaunts in "Around Town:"

Mr. and Mrs. Charles Werly of Powder Point are sunning in Nassau, where they ran into the Carleton Knights and the David Mittells, who remained only long enough to pick up their annual mid-winter tan. Nelson Smith stopped at the Greenbriers in White Sulphur Springs, West Virginia, on his way back from a convention at Hobe Sound, Florida. Dick Mullowney played in a member-guest golf tournament with Frank Pace, former Secretary of the Army, and the Richard Patricks wrote from Johannesburg, Africa, last week. Their Powder Point neighbors, Mr. and Mrs. Ted Berghaus, will fly home from Paris after touring Spain. Mr. and Mrs. John Cutler of Washington Street were in Plymouth Saturday....

There is more fun in running a weekly newspaper than is commonly believed. Assume that you have just launched a weekly in a bedroom community with a population of four or five thousand. You will soon learn there are dozens of clubs and organizations willing—eager, indeed—to elect you unanimously as their public relations director. In your town there will be at least one "social" or meeting of community interest every night, along with morning and afternoon activities. On certain evenings, several meetings whose proceedings are of varying degrees of interest to the community, may be held. Even with the full cooperation of your loving wife, you cannot begin to cover all these gabble or gobble sessions. Why, then, cover any one, unless it is of such general interest as a special town meeting or an open hearing to air a project which will have an impact on the taxpayers' pocketbooks? Cover too many activities and you will wear yourself to a frazzle. Moreover, your presence at some gatherings may not be desired. If an organization wants publicity, it will send in copy.

There is an increasing number of organizations in Duxbury, including Rotarians who own the town, Kiwanians who run it, and Lions who enjoy it. There are at least fifty church groups, along with the Myles Standish Club, the John Alden Society and Society of Mayflower Descendants. In addition to several men's clubs, there is the GAR and the DAR, the Frostbiters, Great Books Club and the Cubs, Brownies, and Girl and Boy, along with Mariner and Sea Scouts. We receive news from all these groups from time to time, and are occasionally asked even to boost the Boosters Club.

Since you cannot cover all activities, why not ask each group to appoint a member to funnel in news? Tell the lad or lassie in charge of public relations to jot down facts and to be sure that all names are correctly spelled.

Editing copy is easy. Give anyone who does a creditable job a by-line, unless he or she is a violet by a mossy brook who objects. To some suburban Boswells, a by-line is as thrilling as having his lighted name on a theatre marquee is to a budding Barrymore.

No matter how much you organize, however, there will always be that Monday rush to contend with, for it is then that most news comes in to be processed for those linotype machines that turn warm words into cold slugs on Tuesdays and Wednesdays. More copy dribbles in on Tuesday mornings, and spot notices may even come in before the last "form" goes to press around noon on Wednesday. Let's tune in again on Bobbie and see how a mother of five used to handle the routine:

Mondays start early for John and me, especially during the school year. In the next bedroom we hear Meg's alarm go off at five-thirty. After our sixteen-year-old daughter dresses and packs her clothes for another week at the day school she attends in Boston, she nudges her Daddy at six o'clock. He often slips on a topcoat or raincoat over his pajamas and drives her to Kingston, where she catches the bus. I doze off, meanwhile, and when John returns he brings me breakfast on a tray. Breakfast is the one meal he cooks well. By this time Gail has returned from Josselyn's with the *Globe* and *Herald*.

Some mornings I let John sleep and enjoy the ride down Bay Road to Kingston as dawn breaks. You can see the color creep into the sky across the bay beyond the strip of land on which is Gurnet Light, and gradually the pasture land along the road takes on a few glints of light. After kissing Meg good-by, I turn back to find the sun just coming up over the horizon, foretelling the weather for the day. Usually I continue past the house to Josselyn's. Although her store does not open until seven o'clock, Mrs. Linde lets me in for a package of doughnuts or English muffins to add to the children's breakfast.

When I get back I find it so peaceful to sit with my cup of coffee on the chaise longue on our glassed-in porch and glance through the papers, checking social notes and death notices. Often, even at this early hour, there will be a knock at the door. It may be a junior executive dropping off a page of news on his way to the city. After finishing my first cup of coffee, I look in the front hall to see if any copy has been left on the table or whether an envelope has been slipped under the door. Well before eight the telephone generally begins to ring. Someone may call in a news item or ask about our rates for classified ads. At any time of day or night people call to ask for odd information. One woman wanted to know when the Truro Centennial was, a man asked who in town collected rubbish (I told her of the person who advertises in the *Clipper*), and another wanted information about a silent auction at a church fair. One night while the harbor was being dredged, a neighbor called: "You would be doing Duxbury residents a great service if you would explain the toots which the dredge makes." I told the gentleman to look in the latest *Clipper* for the piece titled "Whistle Talk." Many others tell us over the phone of our latest error. Our readers, remember, include all town officials, teachers, club directors, doctors and other professional men.

"I was just appointed program chairman for the Dainty Tid-Bits Club," a high school girl may tell me over the telephone. "When do you have to have the news?" The best time, of course, is right after it happens.

By now it's time to get Gail off to school. The phone rings again. Someone is opening a new dog-trimming and shampooing shop. Are there many dogs in Duxbury? she asks. I tell her that there are times when I think there are more dogs than people. The front door opens and I ask the person to come in. The next call is from someone who complains about being billed twice for his last ad. What a boring bit of news to hear

134

before my second cup of coffee. No—sorry, I say. I can't look it up now. Just pay the first bill.

John comes down for breakfast and wants to know what's been going on. Jim Queeny dropped by with the Frostbiters' news and John Murdock brought over a ten-inch real estate ad, I tell him. John is scheduled to spend most of the morning answering the phone and editing copy. Much of it comes in the ten o'clock mail.

The first stop on my rounds is at Hall's Corner. Two ads aren't ready yet. Will pick them up on my way back from Kingston and Plymouth. "O.K., Baby," says Eddie at the Puritan Clothing Company in Plymouth, "here you are." He gives me a half-page mat featuring boys' jackets. "How's John? Tell him I want an autographed copy of that book he's writing when he finishes it." Down the street for a few more stops. "Mr. X is in conference," the girl in the front office says. "Can you come back?" I go down the street for a cup of coffee and saunter through the ten-cent store where I pick up pipe cleaners for John, a lamp shade for the TV room and a pattern for the silk I bought at the sale. If there are no interruptions tonight, maybe I can cut out the pattern. I'd like to have the dress ready for the Wildes' cocktail party Friday.... "Good morning," says Mr. X, now out of conference. "What can I do for you?" He says the mats for his ad haven't arrived. "Can you pick them up tomorrow afternoon?" For the eleventh time I tell him I have to have advertising copy in by Monday night. I suggest that Dr. Y, whose office is across the street, can bring the mats to his home in Duxbury that night. Meanwhile, I ask the size of the ad so we can reserve space for it. I'm so relieved when Mr. X tells me to run the same ad for two weeks. One less stop next Monday....

On the way home I stop at Caldera's Supermarket to pick up the names of the weekly prize winners (even supermarkets need lures these days). The thought of Mrs. Z winning three cases of soda water amuses me. Just what will this abstainer mix it with? And just what will George Q, a bachelor, do with that package of cake mix? The manager of the Drive-In Theatre hands me the weekly ad. "I don't know yet what

135

the feature picture will be," he says. "Can you call after six tonight?"

I check at the post office, since John is often too busy rewriting copy to take time out to get the mail. Friendly exchanges with Fire Chief Eben Briggs and Clarence Walker, who, with his brother, Donald, has taken over the realty business of his father, Percy. While I am getting my mail out of the box, a woman comes over. "Would you mention in the *Clipper* that my daughter made the Dean's List at Skidmore? And, as you know, her brother Bill is majoring in fine arts at Wesleyan." On the way out another woman tells me her daughter has just given birth to a six-pound, eight-ounce daughter, to be named either Kelley Avery Doe or Lydia Raycroft Doe. "Beth and Fred just can't decide." A clergyman comes over just as I, settling behind the steering wheel, am glancing at the stack of mail. "The notice about the JYF trip to the Museum of Science? I don't remember seeing that item." "Sorry," I say. "It probably fell behind the sofa in the TV room." The mail includes a few checks, news, a real estate ad, a turkey ad, a couple of classifieds and mats for a car and telephone ads. Also, the usual number of circulars I should have dumped in the wastebasket in the post office.

John is typing away at the dining-room table. After we have a cup of coffee I drive to Rockland for the full-page food ad. It's ready, as usual. And then a pleasant stop at the counter of the huge supermarket with all its wonderful Italian bread and unusual cheese. The next stop is in Scituate to have a few photographs processed. It's a pretty drive through Norwell, a colonial town that reminds me of Duxbury, with its maples and elms rimming the winding roads, its little streams, farms and old white houses.

Home in time to prepare tomato soup and a jelly sandwich for Ricky. John fixes his own iced coffee, returns from a knock at the front door with a half-page ad. It looks like another good week. Some change from the old days, when we worried if someone dropped a one-inch ad. . . . I go upstairs and start the washing machine in the glassed-in playroom that includes a dryer, ironing board always up and waiting for someone to

136

stumble over, sewing machine, two couches and hundreds of books on the built-in shelves. A glance into the bedrooms reminds me of unmade beds everywhere. The telephone in the playroom rings, and I look around for a pencil and slip of paper. No pencil, so a piece of orange crayon will have to do. I take down a long story about a rummage sale. "Here-after you will have to write out anything like this and send it in," I tell the woman. "Ordinarily we don't take such long notices over the phone." Especially with a stubby crayon, damn it.... "Why? Well, let's just say it's *Clipper* policy. Besides, how else can we be sure names are spelled right, and so on. We like to have copy to check."

I adjust the washing machine, start to make a bed and answer a knock at the door. Mondays! "I'm too tired to think about supper, John," I say wearily. "Would a can of spaghetti and meat balls be all right?"

All during the day, people drop in with news, and some, whom we know well, may sit down over a cup of coffee for a chat. This is one way we pick up items for "Around Town." By evening, John has put a thick bundle of news items and a page of headlines that go with the copy into a large manila envelope. The wastebasket in the dining room is overflowing, and the breakfast and luncheon dishes are piled all over the kitchen table and counters. The butter has been melting and the milk is warm. John has been too busy with the phone and copy to clean up.

A glass or two of sherry gives me the lift I need before preparing supper. By this time the idea of spaghetti and meat balls has lost its appeal. When I get the mail I'll stop at Sweetser's for some steak.

In Sweetser's, genial Louis finishes waiting on a customer before telling me to double the size of his front-page ad and change the store hours. One more detail to remember. He cuts me two pounds of rump steak about an inch and a half thick. Joan joins me at the counter. "Hi, Bobbie. Say, I've lost my dark glasses, so would you put in an ad for me? You know how to word it. Mention that they're prescription glasses, otherwise I wouldn't mind. Want me to pay you now?" She hands me a five-dollar bill, and Louie changes it for me. I hope I remember to give Joan credit.

Once, when John and I were shopping in a supermarket, a Duxbury couple who had run a classified ad for two weeks became separated. The husband, thinking the ad had run only once, handed John a dollar bill. His wife, meanwhile, not knowing he was settling up, paid me for the ad. We finally got the matter straightened out.

"That will be three-forty-nine," Louie is saying.

"You must have cut it from a prize Black Angus bull," I teased. It tasted as if it were.

On my way out a woman whose name I can never remember pays me three-fifty for a nine-month subscription for her daughter, who, she said, is a buyer for a department store in Memphis, Alabama. "Hetty will be here for the holiday," she adds, making me wonder just what holiday she means. I use the three-fifty to pay for the steak, making a mental note to jot down the payment in the day book before I get mixed up. "Let's see," I say tentatively, "I'm awful about names. . . ." She brightens. "O'Malley," she says. "Dan and I bought the Prindle house off Washington Street. You know, the cute little saltbox with the windmill in the back yard. And Dan and I both simply love, we just adore, the *Clipper*. We can hardly wait for Thursday mornings to come."

After assuring Mrs. O'Malley that John and I appreciated such comment, I check the social item I just jotted down on the steak wrapping paper. Oh, certainly, she says. Perfectly all right to use "Hetty."

Things calm down after dinner. We are watching the climax of a mystery drama when the phone rings for the eightieth time that day. "Say we'll call back," I shout up to Gail. Sometimes Ricky gets to the telephone first, for he is a self-appointed *Clipper* editor who upon occasion leadeth the *Clipper* into strange waters. When the chairman of a church supper came to the front door with a front-page ad, Ricky studied her. "Are you a witch?" he asked. Once I walked into the living room just in time to hear him say, as he hung up the phone, "That will be five dollars." Another time he banged the telephone receiver after saying, early Monday morning, "No, it's too late." Gail, who had answered the upstairs phone, rushed down, saucer-eyed. "Mummy! Someone just wanted to know if you would pick up a full-page ad, and Ricky told him it was too late and he hung up." We never knew who the prospective advertiser was.

Well, Monday finally grinds to a halt, and I read in bed before dropping off to sleep.

Thus ends Bobbie's version of those frantic Mondays. The meetings she mentions at the post office and in Sweetser's Store with friends or neighbors who bring her up to date on their families are known to every operator of a country weekly. The editor may be talking to an attendant at a gas station, returning a book to the library or getting a haircut but he is still collecting social nuggets for the "Around Town" column. We pick up many gems at socials. A guest may mention to Bobbie in an aside that she has just returned from New Hampshire, where she visited the Governor, and if pressed for details may add, "Now, please don't put this in the *Clipper*."

"But the *Clipper* isn't just another newspaper," Bobbie may say. "It's a friendly little sheet that tries to keep the townspeople up on one another's activities."

"You know, that's right," one woman told her at a garden party. "I didn't think of it that way, but how right you are. Go ahead and print it."

Then there is Jane Doe, the other extreme. Jane, who cannot understand why her multifarious activities are not pictured in our crystal ball, is slightly puckered when her social hedge-hopping is not reported in the local bugle, although she never bothers to send or phone in news. At a cocktail party, under the gentle anesthesia of a gin and tonic or five, she suddenly bursts into prose. You struggle to store in the recesses of memory all the data she pours into your ear, not daring to pull out a pad and jot down the notes, since you are a guest, not a reporter. There are generally three or four Janes, along with one or two John Does, at a festive party, and if you have a good memory you can be preparing half an "Around Town" column while sipping a cool drink.

There is also the person who collars you when you are in a hurry. If you have thirty seconds to spare as you pause at a red light on the way to the bus stop, just what do you say to that pleasant chap in the car who pulls alongside, winds down his window and asks, "Say, John, do you have a minute?"

"Well, I was planning on making the next bus, and—" Already you have used up twelve seconds.

"Oh, this won't take more than a sec. I just thought you'd like to know that one of the pups our Collie had has a mark on her face that looks like an exclamation point, and—"

"Wonderful, great. Look, Tod, why don't I call you some time tonight." Then you roar off just in time to park your car and jump onto the bus as it revs up its motor.

One afternoon, loaded with two heavy bags of groceries, I was on the way to the back door when a station wagon pulled into the driveway. It was full of the summer accessories the September voyageurs take back with them after summering in Duxbury.

"I just happened to see you as I came down the street," the chic driver said pleasantly, giving the emergency brake an ominous tug that indicated she was in no hurry. I shifted the groceries for better balance.

"Sorry we don't have a pencil, Mrs. Doe," I say. "Who did you say boated that thirty-six-pound striper?"

"Twenty-five pounds," she said, moving her elbow into a comfortable position as she girded herself for the big gush, somewhat in the manner of a giant comber just before it spanks the shore. "Ned's friends would tease him unmercifully if you exaggerated the size of the bass. Actually, I wouldn't have believed it weighed as much as it did—until we had it cut up, of course, that is—and tucked away in the freezer. Let's see, where was I.... Oh, yes, I knew there was something. The Pontpeers and their children—all except Sudie, who is away at Camp Wobbly up near the Gaspé country, you know, for the first week in September—were on the trip, and Sherry, as usual, got sick. Even the drive to Boston bothers her.... They cruised around the islands before dropping the hook at Naushon, I mean Cuttyhunk, and had a perfectly wonderful time, although Timmy drank too much, as usual. Be sure to mention that when Ned was asked where he boated the striper he said, 'East of the buoy.' "

By this time each bag of groceries felt as if a thirty-five-pound striper had been added.

"Well, thanks a lot, Mrs. Doe, and I do appreciate your telling me all the—"

"If you like, you can say that Ned and I have returned to our home in Newton Lower Falls after spending the month of August with Ned's folks—the Perimiters of Bonnie Briarcliffe. You spell Bonnie with an 'ie,' you know, not a 'y.' Ned's father retired just after Christmas, as you probably know. He was treasurer of United Shoelace and—"

"Well, I suppose you'll all be glad to get back to Newton Upper Falls after all our rainy—"

"Lower. Newton Lower Falls."

All right, goddam it, Lower; and I wish you'd hurry back, I tell myself, juggling the loads to give the cheery dame the idea they aren't full of marshmallow fluff. "Well, thanks again, and—"

"Mimi and Godfrey will rent their house to the Squeers of West Acton while they go on a cruise to the West Indies this winter. Mrs. Squeers, as I am sure you must know—Ned says the *Clipper* knows everything that's going on—is the niece of Franny Punnington who used to spend the summer here before her divorce from—"

"Maybe I better set these groceries down, Mrs. Doe," I say, looking helplessly toward the house. Where the hell is Bobbie—vacuuming the damn rug, or something?

"It doesn't make the slightest difference to Ned or me, of course, but if you do have a little extra space you might say that Hammy will be a sophomore at Saint Elmbrook this year, and Deedy will be a senior at Mary Q. Dennison. Incidentally, Deedy spent last weekend down in Quisset—I just love that place, don't you? it's so like Duxbury—with a classmate. Nannie something or other. You can call what's-her-name in the Weed House if you really want her name. Next summer, by the way, Ned and I have taken the Kinnane house on the Nook. With Tod away at that dude ranch in Wyoming, of course, we won't need such a large—" She leaned out of the window of the car when we disappeared from view. "Oh, how awful. It would have to be the eggs, wouldn't it? Well, cheerio, and I do hope you and your lovely wife have a perfectly wonderful winter. Don't forget, it's Newton Lower, not Upper, and West, not East Ayer, I mean Acton."

What a wondrous sound, the roar of the motor that bespeaks the parting guest. There is no pain in my arms or wrists now. They are merely numb. I kick the gate shut.

"By the way, Mr. Cutler, Ned and I want so much to have the *Clipper* sent to us again this year. What are the rates for nine months?"

"Look, could I send you a rate card?" I say sarcastically, but she is too dumb to catch my mood. "The rate is three-fifty as usual."

"Well, we simply couldn't think of doing without that

darling little *Clipper*. And do start with the next issue, won't you?"

This is her way of making sure I get all the blurb about her clan into the paper. Lower, not Upper, Acton, not Ayer, I think to myself as I trudge through the back yard. All I have to do is remember a third of what this dame told me, and Mrs. Seymour will have enough copy for another wastebasket. I was lucky to get away, at that.

There were a few members of her family whom she forgot to mention.

CHAPTER 14

"Put it on the front page, please!"

— ANY PROGRAM CHAIRMAN OF ANY FUNCTION
IN ANY TOWN

Mondays for Bobbie are no longer quite so nerve-shattering, since her friend, Peggy Dunn, now collects the ads, and I continue to edit and rewrite most of the copy unless otherwise engaged.

Today, the *Clipper* often runs to twelve, and occasionally to fourteen pages. We no longer solicit advertising, and except for Peggy Dunn, our Monday assistant, and Miss Ethel McAuliffe, our "country correspondent," we still operate the *Clipper* ourselves. The *Clipper*, which scorns boilerplate more than ever, goes by mail free, as of yore, to all Duxbury boxholders and R.F.D.'s. Although it costs about forty dollars a week to give the paper away, this revenue returns more than twofold in the form of increased advertising income.

Since 1956, I have "ghosted" two volumes of memoirs, cut and abridged another, revised and expanded a fourth and have taken time out to collaborate with Bobbie on this book. Interviews and research for some of my books have taken me as far afield as New York, Pennsylvania, Tennessee, and Mexico City. During my absence—sometimes for two or three weeks at a stretch—Bobbie and her limited staff have never missed a *Clipper* deadline. Indeed, when I return and have the temerity to write or edit *Clipper* copy, Bobbie is apt to be waspish and resentful.

"Go write another book," she said when I returned from one trip.

I felt a desperate need to be wanted. Where was that old feeling of belonging and togetherness between the *Clipper* and me?

"Isn't there *anything* I can do, darling?" I asked.

"You can take Ricky for a walk on the beach," she said. "He's been restless all day. Why don't you pick up some driftwood? It burns with such lovely greenish-blue tints." By this time I was feeling like a piece of driftwood myself. Fortunately, the books still keep me busy, and Bobbie, less cavalier about skippering the *Clipper*, lets me take the tiller now and then.

Tuesdays are usually busy, since either Bobbie or I spend the afternoon at the plant in Braintree reading proofs, checking ads, and writing last-minute copy. The bulk of the copy is taken to South Braintree on Tuesday morning by Chapin Wallour, a Duxbury resident whose office is just a few steps from the Observer Press. Walter Schmitz of the Observer Press or Joe Cavanaugh, his assistant, pick up the copy by

8:30 A.M., and by the time Bobbie or I arrive at the plant early Tuesday afternoon, most of this copy is set. Let's tune in on La Belle Roberta again:

On Tuesday mornings, there are last-minute errands; stragglers drop by with news of club activities, or someone calls about a gold or silver wedding anniversary. The mail brings in some news, including church notes from a minister who never gets his copy in on time. This means that his copy is occasionally left out, if the paper is "full."

After luncheon, I may pick up a stray ad or two on the way to South Braintree. I sit down in the cluttered office and proofread ads first, and then copy. As I proof up the news items, I jot down on a separate piece of paper which stories I want for the front page. These are not always the stories some of the club women want. "Around Town" usually starts on page three and wanders all over the paper, and legals and classifieds go on a certain page, as do church and death notices and the funeral director's four-inch ad, which is inserted once a month to remind the public that his services are still available. It doesn't matter where the rest of the copy goes, since, as John Riley, the gruff but likable foreman says, it's R.O.P. (run of the paper). John and Harold Trufant (Harold once ran his own weekly) put the paper together after Warren Tyler and Bill Rabenaldt set the type: an efficient quartet, who say "throwing your ragbag together is duck soup."

Once in a while, while proofreading, I chuckle at something John has written—he's not always serious—and now and then I spot an error. Mr. X didn't marry Miss Y. . . . He married her sister-in-law. I'm glad I caught that one. "Say, Bobbie," Riley calls in. "What are you going to do with this extra type? It isn't rubber, you know. And where's the head for the lead story? We better set it fourteen-point, since the front page is crowded."

After reading copy for about two hours, I make myself a cup of coffee. "There are doughnuts on the counter, Bobbie," Harold says. "Help yourself." I don't need one, but I take it. "Hey, Bobbie," Warren shouts when I return to the outer office. "Was it B–u–r–t or B–e–r–t who was up at Newfound Lake last week?" I tell him it was Bert. "He and his wife go up there every October; it's about time you knew it." He calls in, "I don't want to know anything about those aristocrats down in that dump."

By 4:30, everything is up, and I lean over the chases watching Riley and Trufant put the *Clipper* together. "Why didn't you say so before?" Riley growls when I tell him to move an ad to the front page. "And look," I add, "don't put those two hardware stores side by side, since they're advertising the same thing." The boys in the shop invariably ask, "Will you have any more copy in the morning?" Not unless there is a murder, I say, or unless the choir soprano elopes with the sexton. At five sharp the clanking of the Mergenthalers and the roar of the presses end abruptly, and the boys scrub the ink off with sand-soap. I pick up the mail on the way home, hope there are some big checks in it.

John, who has been working on a manuscript, almost always asks the same question: "Did you get all the copy in?" I assure him that everything got in except a historical filler that is good any time and some blurb about the scout drive that doesn't start for three or four weeks. "And I left out your long editorial about throwing garbage in the dump. People are tired of hearing you talk about that." He hands me a Tuesday evening special cocktail.

A town dump, as John said in one of his editorials, is a fine institution.

It's an informal meeting place where you run over glass and into people you haven't seen for weeks. It's a place where a person can give vent to so many suppressed feelings. Here Father, forced to curb his congenital urge to flick cigarette ashes on the living room rug, toss his topcoat over a chair or leave dull razor blades on a bathroom window sill, can really let off steam. There's something grimly satisfying about heaving cartons full of mildewed shoes, bent coat hangers, twisted toothpaste containers, broken toys, empty lotion bottles and other kinds onto that inspiring mountain of rubble. This shedding-off process gives you a peculiar sense of renewal.

147

You are about to leave the wonderful dump when you notice a perfectly good dresser. Hmmmm. . . . Some fool, too lazy to glue it together, sand it down and refinish it, probably left it there in a moment of weakness and now wishes he had it back. You glance furtively about to see if anyone is looking. It might take some explaining if that snooty neighbor across the street saw you scavenging, but of course you could hardly call it scavenging when you are retrieving a perfectly good dresser which may be an antique. Boy, will your wife be pleased when she sees the dresser. Just what the kids need for the bedroom.

Yes, a town dump is a fine institution. I just came back from the place, and, as usual, I have a feeling of renewal. It was so much fun heaving those cartons of mildewed shoes, bent coat hangers, lotion bottles—it sure does give a fellow a feeling of satisfaction. And it sure was a relief to get rid of that confounded, rickety, ugly dresser I tripped over every time I tried to move around the cellar. It's stuff like that clutters up a house, but you just try telling your wife THAT, chum.

Actually, the dresser John referred to in this editorial was the one *he* brought from the dump, the scavenger.

Probably no dump has received as much publicity as Duxbury's. Besides several editorials on dumps that have appeared in the *Clipper*, Everett Marston described our local dump for the readers of *Time* Magazine. "The town dump is just a nice place for people to meet, leave trash, vow eternal friendship and go their ways," he said. *Time* Magazine, commenting on his words, added:

In Duxbury's own dump, as in Lincoln's, Hingham's and Wayland's, local citizens who can well afford to pay for garbage removal prefer to haul away the week's trash in their own Chevrolets, Thunderbirds, Chryslers and Volkswagens. Thus, on every Sunday morning gather old friends—and new acquaintances—who dump their stuff, then stay around to exchange gossip, renew friendships and, in a most delicate way, pick up a few worthy items discarded by their neighbors.

In such a way one Hingham widow was said to have furnished her home; a Duxbury mother found a piano that served for music lessons for her four children; a Lincoln housewife found a perfectly usable playpen for her baby. To these dumps, too, come service committees from the League of Women Voters and even local politicians in search of a ready-made audience. On one recent Sunday, a crowd of happy-go-dumping Hingham residents showed up with jugs of martinis and plates of hors d'oeuvres, proceeded to make a three-martini cocktail hour to cap off the dumping chores.

But even the town dump can make for complexities. "Like everything else in this Atomic Age," muses Professor Marston, "our dump is getting organized and is not as informal as it once was. The privilege of taking things has gone." It may not be long before some cheerful martini-toting group, decked out in Sunday-go-to-dumping clothes, will be confronted by the ultimate of barriers: a sign reading NO DUMPING.

John and I have never seen a cocktail party in full sway at the town dump, but it is certainly a social center that provides newsy tidbits for "Around Town." Although we don't usually transact business at the dump, John did run into C. Colby Hewitt one Sunday morning and sold him a monthly ad for the *Clipper*. Colby is a partner of Boit, Dalton & Church of Boston.

Only rubbish—no garbage—is supposed to be thrown into our dump. John is forever warring on garbage-dumpers, whom he calls "ratophiles."

While sipping a Tuesday evening cocktail, John may say I'll have to find room for a death notice. "But don't say Mr. X jumped off the ocean liner. Just write he died suddenly."

"Then I'll have to leave out Rotary or Kiwanis news to make room for the obit," I say. I can see the wheels of his mind turning. "No, leave them in. Omit the 'Selectmen News' this week. People can wait until next week to hear that Roy Parks has discovered three more cases of Dutch elm disease and that Isabelle Freeman attended an auditors' convention."

While John calls Mother to ask her over to supper I pull the left-over lamb out of the refrigerator and thumb through the *Toll House Cookbook* for a recipe for curried lamb.

H-m-m-m-m. . . . It calls for celery, and I have none. . . . Well, it will be just as tasty without celery.

"Anybody home?"

I recognize Mother's invariable salutation. For a person of such originality, wouldn't you think she might vary this greeting with something like, "May I come in?" Since John just called her, she knows someone is home.

"Oh, hello, Mother, how are you? Sit down and I'll be right there."

John gives her a cocktail while I open a can of tomatoes and put them in a baking dish with a few bread crumbs sprinkled with grated Parmesan cheese.

"Aren't you going to join us?" John calls in.

Men think lettuce, cucumbers and dressing will get together all by themselves if left completely unmolested.

I suddenly remember I have to put the clothes in the dryer, since Ricky has no pants for tomorrow, and John is always annoyed when he runs out of handkerchiefs. The phone rings and I pause on the way to tell the person at the other end of the line that it is too late for an ad. "Monday night is our deadline, you know," I say sweetly. Inside I feel tart. He explains that being a new advertiser, he didn't know about deadlines, and is most anxious to get an eight-inch ad in this week's issue. He is opening a new bakery next week, so will I stretch a point and take his ad? I decide to leave out Rotary and Kiwanis. I know most of the members, and they are a jolly group who won't mind. John is so vague he won't even notice their news was omitted.

"Look, Bobbie," he calls in. "You can finish whatever you're doing later. Come on in and sit down." I sit and listen to Mother and John talk about writing this or that, and wonder whether I'll ever write anything except my signature on checks.

When I was running the *Clipper* with less hausfrau interference, the chore of putting it together ended by five o'clock on Tuesdays, except for any important last-minute changes on Wednesday mornings. Bobbie, however, a perfectionist, insists on returning to the Braintree plant for two or three hours every Wednesday morning to check forms after they are ready for the press. She usually finds a few errors, and this makes her happy in the knowledge that her trip was not wasted. While there, she checks final prices in the weekly full-page food ad and runs the subscription stencils through the machine. This used to take me twenty minutes, but she does the job in about five. When the stencils are finished, she sorts the wrappers into geographical bundles, putting, for example, all the Newtons, Brooklines and Wellesleys in one pile. Then she picks up all the copy, ads and mats that may be needed later for checking purposes and pauses for luncheon on the way home. The *Clipper* week is over for Bobbie and me. Robin Starr picks them up late Wednesday afternoon, takes them home and folds them with the help of his brother Gary and Fizz Richards. He also distributes copies to the three stores where they are sold and, finally, delivers them to the central post office before eight o'clock on Thursday morning. Listen again to Bobbie:

Meanwhile the cycle continues. On the street, in stores, or at social gatherings we learn that Peg and Bill have sold their house and are moving to Kansas City. Johnny Jones has just had his tonsils out and Joe Soaks has just left for Reno for the long expected divorce. His wife's affair with the milk man or clerk or painter has been common gossip for some time, and the story goes that he was one of the last to hear of the shabby business. We can't put all these things in the *Clipper*. "Someday," we tell our friends, "we'll put out an unexpurgated edition. And the following day? That's the day we'll leave town."

We have one drawer for news, another for checks, and even Ricky knows which is which. As items come in, they are thrown into the news drawer of the desk in the TV room. If John has a few free minutes on Saturday morning, he types up whatever he finds and mails the copy to Braintree so it can be set on Monday. This seldom takes him more than half an hour. Although he built himself a marvelous two-story studio at the end of the garden, which is equipped with heat, light, and comfortable furniture, he prefers to work at the trestle table in the dining room. The only thing that seems to bother him is the sound of the vacuum cleaner. On Mondays we often sit down at our typewriters at opposite ends of the trestle table. He proofs everything I write: "Why do you say the Evening Alliance will meet for supper tonight at 6 P.M.?" he may say. "That's a *triple* redundancy." And when I write that the refreshments are in charge of Don Cranston, he may give me a withering look and ask whether the refreshments were alcoholic. "That's the only kind of refreshments that I've seen in charge of people. How many times must I tell you to say the person was in charge of refreshments, not vice versa?" He also makes a fuss if I use some such hackneyed phrase as "proud parents" or "bouncing baby." I am learning, although I am still apt to mix up my "e's" and "i's." The children, when home, relieve us of telephone duty. We call back only if necessary. Thus, although *The Duxbury Clipper* has expanded over the years—more than quadrupling its volume of advertising—the over-all operation has become smoother and easier.

Every town has cranks, including those who threaten a poor country editor with violence. When Gail was ten, she was entertaining two young damsels of the same age when a rough-looking stranger came to the front door. Gail couldn't wait to tell me the exciting story:

"I was playing with Vicky Lawson and Janet Sawyer when I heard the knock. When I opened the door, I saw an ugly-looking man who looked awfully dirty. He asked where Mummy and you were, and I told him you wouldn't be home until about six o'clock. After he asked where the *Clipper* was printed and things like that he told us to be sure to lock all the doors and windows in the house because in a little

while a man was coming over to wreck the house. After acting very serious, this bad man left.

"We were quite scared at this, so Janet thought of a plan. This was it: When the bad man came, Vicky would open the door. Then, when the villain drew his gun, Janet, from behind the door, would knock him down by hitting him over the head with a baseball bat. Then I would pick up his gun and point it right at him.

"We waited and waited, and finally Vicky looked out the window and saw a man come. It wasn't the same man, but we had never seen him before. Janet and I hid behind the door, with baseball bats ready while Vicky opened the door and asked the man who he was.

" 'I'm Sheriff McDonald,' he said. 'Is your father at home?'

"The sheriff! All of us were so scared we ran into the kitchen and tried to hide in the broom closet, but the vacuum cleaner was in the way, and there wasn't room for all of us."

"Why were you so afraid of the sheriff, Gail?" I asked. "Why didn't you tell him about the stranger who threatened you?"

Her eyes widened. "Oh, I don't know. You know how it is on television—all those sheriffs and villains. We just got scared, I guess."

Sheriff McDonald, a kindly gentleman, had merely dropped in to leave the notice of a foreclosure to be published in the *Clipper*. He never learned how close he came to being hit over the head with a baseball bat or two.

I was in New York when, around two o'clock on Sunday morning, the *Clipper* phone rang. Robert, then seventeen, explained I was not at home.

"The person sounded sober," Robert said later, "but a little grim. 'We'll be over in a little while to take care of you people,' he said."

Robert piled furniture against all entries, figuring that by the time any intruder passed the barricade, he could call the police. Nothing happened, however, leaving one more unsolved mystery. We studied recent issues of the *Clipper*, looking for some inflammatory item. There had been a spirited contest for the school committee, and the telephone call came a few hours after election results were in, but the *Clipper*, as usual, had not taken sides in the campaign.

Debunking cherished myths can be hazardous in a historic town proud of its landmarks, but there are enough persons interested in setting the record straight to justify the practice. The story of the Pilgrims landing on Plymouth Rock is one challenged by many competent historians.

"This story," we noted in an early *Clipper*, "dates only to 1769, when the Old Colony Club of Plymouth was formed. Ephraim Spooner said that when he was six, he heard Ruling Elder Thomas Faunce, 95, say that his father told him the Pilgrims used the rock as a stepping stone. But Bradford, Winslow and other contemporaries made no mention of the

Rock, and sailors ask why a shallop should be driven to a rock for a landing when the Town Brook was nearby."

This evidence may not have made as many converts to a less glamorous account of the historic landing as it might have in Brooklyn, but it was generally greeted as an interesting sidelight to a legend. In connection with Plymouth Rock—and long may it stand as a symbol, unhacked by tourist machetes—the *Clipper* quoted a whimsical remark we heard an exchange student from Wales make to a Plymouth Duxbury audience:

"I am not too sure whether it would not have been better for Plymouth Rock to have landed on the Pilgrims instead of vice versa." Instead of being forthwith placed in the stocks, he drew polite, if mild, applause; for local descendants of those sturdy Pilgrims take such touches of whimsy in stride, justifiably proud of their courageous forebears. The debunking, rather than damaging the repute of the *Clipper*, increased its unpaid circulation around the country. Professor John H. Casey was right when he said a weekly newspaper "is read longer by more members of the family."

The first proof of this came toward the end of 1950 when a professor at Hilyer College in Connecticut wrote:

While on a brief visit to the old home town last weekend, a friend gave me several back copies of your paper. I was impressed by its several attractive qualities. The diversity of the reading material and its above-standard literary qualities were two of its virtues which impressed me. . . .

A few weeks later there was more evidence that the *Clipper* was making the rounds: "You might like to know," a reader said, "that at least one copy of the *Clipper* travels far. Julia Smith of Powder Point, after reading her copy, mails it to her sister, who is a nurse in Tokyo. Nora (the nurse) then sends it to Mrs. Frank Martin, formerly of Duxbury, and she, in turn, mails it to Bradford Bennett in Korea. By the time Brad passes it around, it is apt to be frayed." An Army sergeant in Spokane wrote: "I have just finished reading several issues of your fine newspaper. It reaches us through my daughter (who also lives in Spokane) who receives it from her aunt in Duxbury after the latter's family reads it."

It gradually dawned on us that this chummy routine was cutting into our paid circulation. We did something about this alarming state of affairs when this note was published in "Sounding Off:"

The *Clipper* certainly gets around. I send my copy to my daughter in Scarsdale, New York, who sends it to a friend in Elmira who mails it to a friend in California who forwards it to her sister in Tucson, Arizona, who finally passes it on to her son who is at an air base in Greenland—all interested in our good old town.

In an appended editorial parenthesis we noted: "Next step: get all these good people interested in *Clipper* subscription rates."

Mrs. Olive V. Saunders of Washington Street doesn't believe in sending the same *Clipper* around. She has cultivated the charming hobby of sending the *Clipper* to any friends who move, and to give an idea of the scope of her operations, her latest subscription is for a friend who settled in Palembang, Sumatra.

Concerned with the reception *The Duxbury Clipper* would have, Bobbie and I were delighted to get such a flood of encouraging letters. It was not, however, all hearts and flowers. While feeling a warm glow of satisfaction, we gradually became aware of our responsibility to the public.

CHAPTER 15

"Investigate the brand of local politics to determine whether you wish to become mixed up (as inevitably you will) in local political affairs. It would certainly be foolish for you to settle in an area where your political theories would not fit."

—THE GOVERNMENT BROCHURE

The first community skirmish in which the *Clipper* became involved occurred early in 1951 when rival groups tried to take over the Duxbury Playhouse, which by then had failed, following scandalous reports about its managing personnel. The storm lowered in February when an articulate duenna whom we shall call Mrs. Dithers (she often thus referred to herself) sounded off. Mrs. Dithers, plumping for a community theater, castigated the summer theater operators who were trying to take over the spacious playhouse with its revolving stage:

"The vultures are waiting," she wrote in "Sounding Off." "Like scavengers circling a dying animal, commercial interests are getting ready to take over the Duxbury Playhouse."

She argued, the town had a wonderful potential in the best physical equipment of any summer theater in New England, along with widespread community interest and support. "This has come to the attention of the people of talent and stature in one of the best community theater projects in New England. We can get help. We can fulfill the promise that is inherent in the dream and hope of the Duxbury Playhouse. If we save the Playhouse from its immediate financial crisis, we can get help and really get it solidly established in a community theater."

Two Duxbury groups locked horns. The group who wanted the community theater had approximately three thousand dollars pledged from three hundred supporters when they enlisted the aid of a Duxbury banker who assured them he could raise an additional amount that would bring the total in the "save-the-theater" kitty to fifteen thousand dollars. That was the sum, according to Mrs. Dithers and her followers, that would guarantee victory over the "vultures."

A second group, with solid backing from affluent trustees of the Duxbury Playhouse, favored a music center, where opera would alternate with drama. The eventual dream was to make summer Duxbury another Tanglewood.

The air was full of charges and countercharges by the spring evening when two ministers—one of whom had a local pulpit—woke Bobbie and me on their way home from an emergency meeting of the executive council of the "Save-the-Theatre-Committee." The group, we wearily learned, needed seven thousand dollars more as an absolute minimum to make possible the opening of the Playhouse for the 1951 season. This money had to be raised by March 31 to meet the most

158

pressing obligations to creditors for taxes, bank interest, and the initial expenses of launching the enterprise.

They asked for *Clipper* support in the drive for the seven thousand dollars. A short time later we reported in the lead story:

At least 320 Duxbury residents have declared themselves in favor of making the Duxbury Playhouse a genuine community theater. Most of them have contributed a dollar or more, eager that the fund should be raised to open the Playhouse this season under the direction of David Tutaev, brilliant and widely known artistic director of Boston's Tributary Theatre. The goal is near enough so that contributors may consider themselves charter members of the Playhouse Association. In the nonprofit organization soon to be set up, all contributors regardless of the size of their contributions will have one vote in the election of the directing body.

We explained that Tutaev's training was with the Old Vic Civic Theatre in London, and that, according to Louis Calhern, "some day the Tributary Theatre would turn into the most influential theatrical organization in New England." We did everything we could think of to promote the project for Duxbury, in Duxbury, by Duxbury.

It was at this time that a local banker guaranteed Mrs. Dithers and her friends enough money to take over the Duxbury Playhouse. A meeting was called to discuss the deal, with representatives from the two rival groups attending. The issue was decided by the directors of the old Duxbury Playhouse, who voted for the music and drama venture. Although well received at first, it finally failed, after operating at a deficit.

"What a long way we have gone from our efforts to establish a community theater," a crusader for the community theater said in "Sounding Off" in 1951, following a gloomy financial report issued by The Plymouth Rock Center of Music and Drama.... "The point that needs to be made is that this group (the devotees of music and drama) is what the Playhouse board of directors chose in the face of the clearly expressed will of more than three hundred Duxbury people for a community theater, plus the offer of fifteen thousand dollars to buy the Playhouse for such a project." We were puzzled by her final sentence, in view of the support we had given the enterprise she favored: "I hope you will be *allowed* to print this."

"Caught my wife in an allowing mood," I wrote.

Bobbie and I soon learned that a weekly editor gets involved in any controversy that rocks a community. A mild protest about a trivial matter will lead to spirited and prolonged sounding off.

"We moved to Duxbury in January, 1951," a reader wrote, "and have gone to church since March, yet no one from the church has called to welcome us either to the church or to Duxbury. It is strange in comparison with the way other towns and cities have welcomed us when we lived in their midst."

After a few heated exchanges, a minister's wife remarked:

The minister's wife is probably the one person in a parish able to see both points of view. The writer of the *Clipper* letter makes it seem that a newcomer may sit and wait to be discovered by some clergyman and will then attend the church of the one who reaches him first. One doesn't wait for the doctor or dentist to come to announce his availability. Nor do many choose their church on such a basis. Newcomers are more apt to say, "I am so and so, living at such and such address. I am a Unitarian from Metopia, and would like to have you call and tell me about your church and its school."

Since a weekly should be a forum for its readers, most letters should be printed, provided they conform to the canons of good taste. By publishing some letters, however, the editor is shaking a hornet's nest. There was some sizzling repartee when one elderly lady, with a pen as vigorous as it was eloquent, pounced on the "trick or treat" tradition of Halloween: "In principle," she said, "it's the same as the gangster blackmail that demands 'protection money' from a laundry in lieu of having acid thrown on the clothes." Another storm lowered when an equally eloquent resident attacked Duxbury High School for its policy of permitting seniors to solicit money from the community for their yearbook. The upshot was that seniors now dream up projects that enable them to pay for the yearbook themselves.

From time to time *The Duxbury Clipper* sponsors a feature to increase reader interest. Our "Vocabu-Ladder" competition and "Mystery House" contests were so successful, we announced an essay competition whose theme would be "A New High School for Duxbury." A timely topic, indeed, with all those superheated comments that had been running in "Sounding Off." Duxbury, like every other American community, had its quota of angry citizens who considered a school gymnasium or auditorium a frill, and a few mossbacks who regarded any new school building itself as an unnecessary frill.

"The essays," we said, "must not exceed three hundred words. They will be judged for thought, grammar, and originality of expression. Judges are Professor William Maulsby, Professor Everett Marston and Miss Margaret Elliott. All prize-winning essays will be published in the *Clipper*."

Superb judges, Bobbie and I agreed. Maulsby, a former staffer on *The Christian Science Monitor*, had taught journalism at the University of Pittsburgh; Marston, author of the novel *Take the High Ground*, taught English and was official historian of Northeastern University. Miss Elliott, a former school teacher, was also able and respected. Nobody, of course, could possibly challenge their competence or integrity. Of course not.

Mary Emerson, fifteen, was complimented on her winning piece, whose theme was that tomorrow never comes. "If construction of a new high school is continually put off until tomorrow, not only will building costs become astronomical, but Duxbury students will lose out." One of Mary's concrete suggestions was "sound-proof music rooms" where the band could blare away with no invasion of privacy. "No insult to the band intended," she added.

Equally innocuous and well written was David Benson's essay that took second prize. Then came theme number three, authored by Robin Starr. Concentrating on the matter of convenience for students, he noted that under "existing cramped conditions, students have no place to put articles which do not fit in their small desks." Then came his block-buster: "There has been a great demand for a student smoking room or perhaps some kind of concrete law set down permitting smoking in certain places. . . . It would seem that if upwards of one million dollars can be spent on a new school, a few hundred dollars could be sacrificed for the personal wants of the students."

"I hardly remember being more shocked than at the suggestion in the piece on the projected high school that a student smoking room be considered," wrote the woman who had denounced the "trick or treat" tradition. "That the school would think of encouraging addiction to smoking on the part of teenagers so they could not go through a school session without indulging themselves seems the nadir of decadence."

Furious taxpayers phoned Bobbie and me asking why the three judges had unanimously voted to award a prize to such

162

a dastardly proposal. We explained that the views expressed by Robin reflected neither those of the judges nor the *Clipper*. "Miss Elliott, for example, neither smokes nor condones the practice among teenagers." Some of the loudest wails came from sanctimonious fathers who, we suspected, as youngsters used to grind up birch leaves and roll them in brown paper to make cigarettes when corn silk was not available.

"We don't agree with Robin Starr's proposal," we said, "but his well-expressed thoughts indicate that he has the courage to say what other students have been thinking. The problem is recognized by some prep schools. In certain schools, smoking is taboo. In others, it is permissible with parental approval, but only at supervised times in supervised places." We added that some parents recognized the fact that since Junior will smoke down in the boiler room, out in the woods or behind the shed, "he might as well do it under proper supervision." We added that "in no part of his essay did Robin state or imply that the school would think of encouraging addiction to smoking on the part of teenagers so they could not go through a school session without indulging themselves."

"In regard to your comment on my letter," the elderly woman shot back, "a teenager who cannot get through a school session without smoking is certainly an addict. A school that provides a place for him to indulge in this habit is certainly encouraging his addiction."

Another resident, commenting on our statement that the prize was given solely on the basis of literary merit, asked whether we thought the novel *Lolita* had merit—"literary merit," that is.

"We do, indeed," we answered, "as do so many of Emile Zola's novels, some of which are more shocking than *Lolita*."

Another annoyed reader castigated us for writing "Xmas" in a headline. Pointing out that the practice of spelling "Christmas" in the abbreviated form was older even than Duxbury, we said: "The ancient Greeks wrote Christ as 'Expistos,' pronouncing it 'Christos,' and the early Christians used 'X' to represent Christ." We added that "Xmas," a respectful word, often fits better into newspaper heads than the longer form. That got us off the hook.

Another reader advocated a practice akin to an attack on motherhood:

> If a dog has no license tag, I say shoot him. Cats are one of our worst game and rabbit destroyers and no one controls these pests. The best cure for this condition is a charge of 63. It's open season the year round on these pests.

The previous week, in an editorial on dogs headed "*Cave Canem*," we had mentioned the responsibilities of dog owners. We suggested no such brisk program, however, as shooting man's best friends. Accordingly, we appended these words to Irate Citizen's alarming epistle:

> We sharply disagree with the sentiments expressed in this letter. Shoot unlicensed dogs, indeed! Penalize a dumb animal because its owner is derelict in his duty? Shall we ask the dogs whether they are unlicensed 'with the consent of owner'? If we start shooting dogs and cats because they are nuisances, where shall we stop? There are moral as well as legal laws.

Another reader took on the Police Department and American Legion in one frontal assault. To celebrate July Fourth, Duxbury has an elaborate celebration, complete with parade, fireworks display and a midway. Some of the younger Legion members became so enamored of Duxbury Days, they expanded festivities to a four-day celebration. One feature was the midway, and, when the police were not looking, there was spin-the-wheel gambling. It was the type of gambling often practiced at county fairs. Nevertheless, the articulate taxpayer objected:

I am in complete favor of having such a celebration, but not of the sort which has been inflicted on us this year. I refer to the concessions and the flagrant gambling which seem to flourish with the apparent approval of our own police department, to say nothing of the sanction of the American Legion officers and committee.

She added:

I dislike having my house used as a comfort station and of being insulted and cursed when I refuse to let persons who have obviously been drinking come in.... This morning I picked up corn cobs, sticky papers, beer cans and bottles, and three obscene articles directly in front of my front door.

She also reproved the Selectmen for failing to report to the town all hidden costs involved in the celebration.

The suggestions she and others made have eliminated most of the unsavory aspects of our annual celebration, which includes the biggest bonfire on the South Shore. In 1959, Duxbury Days was featured on Dave Garroway's morning television show "Today," as typical of the nation's Independence Day celebrations.

Bobbie and I have often been asked to serve as judges in various contests, including the annual Tournament of Plays at Duxbury High School. A few years ago the Legion appointed me chairman of judges in the beauty contest in which "Miss Duxbury Days" is crowned. When the finalists narrowed down to three comely daughters of dear friends or neighbors, I sneaked out a rear entrance and quickly pressed into service an elder of the community known for his cool analytical judgment and tact, and unknown to the lovely maidens and their families. A cowardly but strategic maneuver, born of necessity. In the *Clipper* account the name of the elder statesman replaced mine in the list of judges.

We don't mind the operational hazards of running a paper. Some fellow parishioners invariably stir up a mad if our editorial is strong, and if it's sizzling, there may be those who hate you for life. Even a quip may arouse ire. When our waterfront reporter became negligent in his reports of a local bass derby, a reader asked who won the derby.

"The bass," we said, and that was enough to goad our miffed reporter into action.

Another time we were criticized for failing to print scores of a cribbage tournament. "I am near the top of the standing and see no reason why this should be kept a secret," a player wrote. "By the time word gets around, I expect to drop into seventh place, since my partner is a slow thinker."

"There are several theories," I explained. "One is that the scorekeeper is in last place."

This brought a sally from Irked Scorekeeper: "In replying to Irate's letter about cribbage scores, let me say that at the end of the first period of the tourney no one knew whether they were standing or sitting, including the scorekeeper. This happened when one team dropped out. Now we are back in the groove. Irate is correct—I am still near the bottom."

When a reader sarcastically inquired, "Do hick editors make enemies?" we answered, "Oh, no. But you can say of a hick editor what Whistler said about Oscar Wilde: 'He has no enemies, but none of his friends like him.'"

Often a dash of whimsy is all that is needed to placate an aggrieved member of the community who writes a complaining letter.

"As a new resident," one wrote, "may I ask if it is customary to register gentle reproof if beer bottles are found on certain mornings strewn on my otherwise decorative lawn?"

"Permissible," we said, "only if the bottles are non-returnable."

Friendly give-and-take in a reader's column adds a little paprika if a genial mood is maintained. In one issue we noted that our friend Earl Russell took his daughter Hope skating on a cranberry bog.

"While you're putting on your skates," Earl said, "I'll make sure the ice is safe. It was, until Earl reached a place where he fell in up to his waist. According to our latest dispatch, Earl is trying to exchange his skates for a waffle iron."

This drew a comment from Providence, Rhode Island: "Being an infrequent visitor to Duxbury these days, it's nice to get your newsy publication. Don't tell me Earl Russell is still falling into ponds?"

Reference was to a summer lawn party when Earl, by mistake, backed into a fish pond. "I wouldn't have minded," he said, "except that my martini glass was full."

When we asked who the Duxbury owner of Massachusetts license plate Number One was, a resident sounded off: "Anyone who knows anything knows Massachusetts plate Number One belongs to Dr. Tudor of Adams Street, Milton."

A letter published the following week needled this snob: "Anyone who *really knows* anything knows Massachusetts plate Number One belongs to Dr. Tudor of Randolph Avenue, Milton."

"Thanks," I wrote, "for putting that other Miltonian in his place."

The oldtimer gave snobs short shrift:

"I remember the gink, Snoop-Scoop. Belonged to one of them snooty-tooty clubs in Boston. It was so uppity the doorman give you a glassy eye if you spoke to him without bein' introduced by Henry Cabot Lowell and your name ain't in the social cash register."

"Now, let's see, what club could that be?" the roving reporter said. "Certainly not the Union or Algonquin."

"It begins with winter, I think, Snoop."

"You must mean the Springset Club, oldtimer."

"It's what I'm tryin' to tell you, son. One night they is a 16-alarm fire. All the fire injuns git there fast and try to bust past this doorman. He stands there, chokin' with smoke, kin hardly speak, tears runnin' down his cheeks from the smoke. 'Sorry, gentlemen,' he says, 'you'll have to use the service entrance.'"

"That story is true, oldtimer, but no doorman was involved. The firemen used the service entrance simply because it was more convenient."

"Like I say, hard days comes on this gink and the come-down is he is so broke he has to work slingin' steak in a—"

"Look, oldtimer, I have to cover a Halloween taffy-pull. Will you get to the point?"

"One day one of them Springset people catches him in this greasy-spoon restaurant. 'What, Ellery,' he says, 'you workin' here?'

"'I work here,' Ellery says. 'But I don't eat here.'"

Noting one day that a resident had run over an otter in Duxbury, we asked whether any other unusual animals had been recently seen.

"Are you asking whether there are any otters or other animals to run over?" a wildlife lover reproved. "Personally, I have quite a long list of interesting animals—and uninteresting people—that I have not yet run over."

"Would like to compare lists with you some time," I said.

There is a time for levity and a time for serious palaver. It's no time for banter when an issue comes up that is of interest to taxpayers. In small towns, even the matter of laying a new sidewalk may be a matter of concern.

The *Clipper*'s basic argument against laying black-top sidewalks with curbing was the cost and the destruction of the rural character of the town. With the approval of the town fathers, the program for sidewalk construction along Washington Street had been under way for eighteen years when we suggested that no further work be done along this line.

The Selectmen may have been unanimous about the need for a Washington Street sidewalk [we editorialized], but Washington Street residents and others certainly are not. Many feel as Pauline Winsor Wilkinson did in 1921 when she wrote: "If the time ever comes when the earth sidewalks with grassy edges are replaced by asphalt with stone copings, I am thankful I shall not see it. It is the Old Duxbury I remember and love." When we think of all those sidewalk-less streets in Duxbury which don't even have cow-paths for pedestrian protection, we wonder why Washington Street, which already had its grassy-edged, rustic sidewalks quite in harmony with the surroundings, needs another.

Washington Street residents joined the fray. One agreed with our stand, remarking that nobody wanted Duxbury to become another Westchester County suburb. A neighbor took issue:

I like sidewalks, not cowpaths. We should think more of elderly people who must walk and mothers who must push baby carriages than whether a few people like the looks of sidewalks. Many of us Washington Street residents want and will get sidewalks.

This was such a crisp, clean debate, we kept it simmering:

Duxbury, unlike a Westchester suburb, is a green-thumb, expose-the-old-beam, fireplacy and Dutch-oveny community that is rustic, but not bucolic; homespun, but not homely. It is a woodsy town with deer walks, private bird sanctuaries and duck-blinds—a town with sprawling forests where cows can get lost. It would take more than a black sidewalk on Washington Street to make a West-chester suburb out of Duxbury, true, but remember that a journey of a thousand miles begins with one step. The sidewalk on our main street in the pre-asphalt era was not, and its remains are not, cowpaths. Mothers with children of baby-carriage age queried said it was no hardship to push prams on the dirt sidewalk, and surely the packed-down dirt surface is easier on the feet of the elderly than asphalt.

Whenever we really want to wrap up an issue, we summon the wisdom of our oldtimer. Here's a snatch of dialogue between him and Snoop-Scoop:

"How come you're soaking your feet in hot water, oldtimer?" the roving reporter asked.

"Wal, you would too, son, if you walked on that aspfault sidewalk on St. George Street. I heard of the dandelions growin' in the cracks so I figgered I got to see for myself. Sure enough, I seen dandelions and moss, too. And, son, that patched-up wavy black ribbon with its chipped curb is so hilly in places I chewed gum to git used to the changin' altitudes. In places it slopes down soze I listed to port. Sergeant Larry Doyle sees me wobblin' and stops to ask if anythin' is wrong." He reached for a towel. "I seen two women pushin' baby carriages on the road, the sidewalk was so rough in places."

"You figure the sidewalk they're talking about on Washington Street is ill advised, then?"

"Snoop-Scoop, if these ginks want a sidewalk, why don't they buy Curley's Folly over there on Route 139 and move it here? Course, I dunno. Mebbe it'd be cheaper to move Duxbury over to Route 139." He scratched his head. "Been buildin' the durn thing since Hector had kittens, this Washington Street sidewalk. Snoop, by the time it gits to the flagpole you and me will be ten feet under and the first part of the sidewalk will be all wore out. Sure it makes sense. Nonsense, that is. And why is it on one side of the street in one place and acrost the street in other places, hey? Which side they goin' to finish in three hundred years—hey, Snoop-Scoop?"

"You have me there, oldtimer."

"Nice little salt-water town like this, country-like and friendly, and them fellers is tryin' to make it into another Bermudy. Son, I like walkin' as good as this Henry Cragin Walker feller. And when they put them aspfault sidewalks in the woods round here the only place left to walk will be Joe Collins' woodlot."

When the smoke cleared, Pauline Winsor Wilkinson would have been pleased with the results. For half a dozen years, now, there have been no new asphalt sidewalks with curbings or stone copings to add an incongruous touch to Duxbury's quaint, winding, narrow streets.

This controversy was mild compared with the heat of battle generated by a zoning proposal. This issue led to the liveliest town meeting since the memory of latter-day descendants of John Alden and Myles Standish runneth not to the contrary.

CHAPTER 16

"The real newspaper is not a mere retailer of news, to be sold as merchandise. The newspaper is the lawyer of the people."

—WILLIAM RANDOLPH HEARST

$\mathbf{A}$ country newspaper can be an important asset to the community it serves only if it keeps the people informed about matters affecting their welfare and pocketbooks.

The weekly editor in a hurry to blast away before learning his way around the labyrinths of his community, will soon come a cropper. It is just as important for him to become familiar with a community's problems as its history and local traditions. Bobbie and I learned one rule at the outset—

never editorialize on the special pleadings of a group unless thoroughly informed on all facts behind a controversy.

Readers in most small towns expect guidance in forming opinions. The editor's job is not to do their thinking, but rather to provide information and stimulus for them to do their own thinking. A weekly newspaper, said John P. Lewis, publisher of the weekly Franklin (New Hampshire) *Journal-Transcript*, must serve as a "unifying force to develop a sense of community. It needs to be a mirror that will throw extra light on the obscure, and into the dark corners."

Mr. Editor should remember two statements. The first, made by Marcus Aurelius over seventeen centuries ago, is: "What is good for the swarm is good for the bee." The second was a bit of practical advice offered by Herbert Bayard Swope after a long career of journalism during parlous times: "I have no formula for success, but I have one sure formula for failure—try to please everyone."

In pre-*Clipper* days, Bobbie and I were often confused on, or had a hazy notion of, many community issues. Nobody clearly stated the point in question so the townspeople could honestly judge it for themselves. It was often difficult to get the electorate to back a project simply because they did not understand it. Once the *Clipper* was launched, we were forced to familiarize ourselves with bed-rock issues.

These issues are resolved at the annual town meeting or at special town meetings. Since our annual March town meetings do not begin until one o'clock on Saturday afternoons, and because it is traditional to complete all town business during this single session, there is little time for deliberation even of such important items as a proposed million-dollar school.

At town meeting, taxpayers vote on "Articles of the War-

173

rant." The Park Department may want a new tractor, the Police Department a new cruiser. Town employees may request a wage increase, and a group of taxpayers may petition for street lights. Duxbury, like other New England towns, is fortunate in having a Finance Committee to supplement the work of its three Selectmen.

The town's nine-man Finance Committee—easily the most important in the community—studies every proposal carefully and makes concrete recommendations at the annual town meeting. Usually their recommendations are followed, although there have been occasions when it was unwise to heed some of their recommendations which were penny wise and pound foolish. It's the editor's duty to study their proposals, along with those made by the Selectmen and other town committees. The editor may find the Selectmen disagreeing with the Finance Committee on certain items. The Finance Committee, for instance, may insist on holding the line at any cost, even if this means doing without a vital service. Here the editor must heed the warning of his old pal, Marcus Aurelius, translating the aphorism into a workable rule: "Does the proposal serve the greatest good of the greatest number?"

A country editor must look behind and beyond the issue. He should remind his readers that if street lights are installed there will be continuing expenses connected with their maintenance. In view of its economy, can a town afford to extend water mains or put in sewers? A vocal group has suggested that instead of adding a wing to the elementary school, double sessions should be inaugurated. At this point the editor should give a graphic account of what double sessions would mean to a housewife who, say, has four children in four different grades. She gets so dizzy trying to get Billy to one bus and meet Nancy at another bus stop, she thinks she is running into herself as she scurries around. Our long editorial on double sessions, reprinted in pamphlet form, was used by the school committee and superintendent as a persuader at an open hearing. We were also pleased when an editorial we wrote on zoning was read aloud at a town meeting in Dedham, Massachusetts.

As editor of the *Clipper*, I study the Articles of the Warrant to be acted upon at town meeting, and try to clarify any thorny issues. I also convene the *Clipper* advisory board to get a cross-section of community ideas. A typical meeting, which is scheduled in time for the *Clipper* to make its own recommendations before town meeting, would include one Selectman; the chairman of the Finance and School Committees, and the Planning Board; the School Superintendent, Water Commissioner, Board of Health agent and an engineer and architect, if a proposed new school, say, is the issue. Two citizens who have been scalding each other in the "Sounding Off" column, are invited to present their views, and in this way, an agreement is frequently reached. After listening to all shades of opinion, the editor will make definite recommendations which, since they appear in his editorial column, are recognized as his own. We rarely differ with the Finance Committee.

At one special town meeting the town was to be asked to buy fifteen acres of land adjacent to property already owned by the town. When the Finance Committee unanimously vetoed the proposal, we found ourselves in the embarrassing position of having to disagree:

If the town wants this land it must buy it now. Failure to do so would be a regrettable blunder. Duxbury, after all, can only gain from this transaction. It cannot lose, for the land in question will increase in value, and the town's equity will be improved.

We added that the loam alone was worth the purchase price, went on to say:

The penny wise say this is enough land to take care of any school expansion or possible future town offices, library expansion, playground facilities or other contingencies that may arise in the next ten or twenty years. NUTS.

When the *Clipper* advisory committee convened on the following Sunday, one member reproved us for the indignity of our concluding word of bluntness. " 'Nuts' is not a nice word," he said.

The townspeople voted overwhelmingly in favor of buying the land, and it turned out to be a sound decision. Today that parcel of land is part of the site to be used for Duxbury's new high school. It was necessary, indeed, to buy more adjacent land for this project.

The day after the special town meeting, one elder statesman on the Finance Committee phoned to blast the effrontery of our editorial which, he said, "in one fell swoop undercut weeks of work of the Finance Committee." After a bit more sound and fury, he added: "In protest, I am resigning from the Finance Committee."

Town meeting itself, a living example of grass-roots democracy in action, is usually an enjoyable interlude in small towns where the townspeople from every nook and inlet congregate to settle town affairs.

Duxbury's meetings are for the most party gay-tempered and conducted in the finest tradition of an old New England institution that gives every taxpayer a right to sound off and vote according to the dictates of his conscience. It is amusing to note how unpredictable voters are apt to be. They may vote through a proposal to build a million-dollar school with scarcely a murmur, then spend ninety minutes arguing over the momentous issue of buying a new lawn mower for the Park Department.

176

The town meeting of March, 1951, we wrote, was a carefree occasion:

It was a quippy afternoon with the whimsy-makers taking the play from the tub-thumping pulpiteers and soap-box messiahs. Francis Perry was in rare form, as was our town moderator. In making certain recommendations in behalf of the Finance Committee, of which he is chairman, Francis reminded the four hundred taxpayers present that he really didn't hate children, old folks or people in general. After some passionate but polite oratory by Isabelle Freeman (our town accountant), all he could say was, "I have neither the will, the wisdom nor the time to answer." Then, when Isabelle's eloquent and humorous plea for a much-needed calculator was denied, Francis added, "I think I'll make myself scarce around Town Office." He kept glancing toward the rear exit to be sure he could make a quick getaway if necessary.

Miss Freeman, after noting that the Assessors' office had been obliged to rent a calculator, added:

It happened that we were able to keep the machine for four months, but only through the entertaining of the girls in the office was this possible.

Feeling this ambiguous statement needed clarification, we wrote:

Our police reporter queried Isabelle after she simmered down. She explained that the calculator had been rented for only a month, but that nobody had come to pick it up until three months later. "When the man did show up he tried to charge us for four months, but Dorothy Boland and I said it wasn't our fault that he hadn't taken the machine before. We finally got him in a good mood by driving him around town pointing out historic sites, and he went away happy."

When four hundred dollars was appropriated for a new "lowering machine" for the Cemetery Department, the moderator innocently asked whether this machine would raise as well as lower, and suddenly a macabre theme became a cheery discussion. "I think we should give Isabelle her new calculator," said a former moderator. "After all, we have appropriated money for a modern device to lower ourselves to our last rest, so there is no reason we cannot appropriate money for a modern device to raise money."

When Fire Chief Eben Briggs complained that his five-hundred-dollar portable lighter had been turned down, a speaker arose: "You would have gotten it if you had asked for twenty-five hundred," he said. In his plea for the lighter, Howard Clark, one of the town's most forcible orators, concluded: "To the dickens with poverty; give the cat another herring."

Dr. Richard Field arose to ask the moderator what he did with his annual salary of forty dollars, and whether he would accept a five per cent increase.

"I spend it on my wife's birthday and Christmas presents," the moderator said, "so a raise might be out of order."

"Can the moderator rule the moderator out of order?" Dr. Field asked.

Dwelling on the unpleasant characteristic of greenhead flies, Howard Clark was asked by the moderator how far out they chased him when he went cruising. "Exactly half a mile beyond Gurnet Light," Howard said, deadpan.

In a dramatic gesture calculated to convince the voters that his proposal would cost each taxpayer only twelve cents [we reported], Nick LaGreca flung a twelve-cent cigar over his shoulder and said: "That's all it would cost you—one cheap cigar." We wish we could add that the story ended here. It did not. During an intermission the *Clipper* political reporter found Nick under a seat looking for his cigar.

Town meeting is occasionally the scene of the perfect squelch. After one windy orator sat down, a fellow parishioner arose and came right to the point: "And now," he said, "let's hear from someone who knows what he's talking about."

A sarcastic taxpayer got his come-uppance after he asked, "Just what is the relationship between the Fire Department and the Forest Fire Department? Why do we need two departments?"

"They are first cousins once removed," the moderator said. "Chief Briggs told us he is equally fond of both, since they are old flames of his."

Then there is Mr. Earnest Citizen who lets his emotions run away with his intelligence. "Duxbury," said one old gentleman, his voice quivering with pride, "has the finest Police Department in the United States." Chief O'Neil and his men grinned at this tribute. Every taxpayer, on the other hand, accepts one statement, often made, at face value: "Duxbury is the finest residential town in the United States." It was at the 1951 annual town meeting that we first heard that remark. Would you like a list of our realtors, dear reader?

All is not levity at this annual convention, however, for it is here that Duxbury is shaped and molded, here that a dangerous pressure group can enact legislation that may mar the character of the town. If every demand for new services were granted, the tax rate would soon soar to a confiscatory level. Town meeting is basically a serious occasion.

It is especially serious when such a proposal as zoning is brought up. The father of Duxbury's excellent zoning system was Percy Walker. Typical of remarks he made at town meeting on several occasions was: "Let's not make Duxbury like one of those towns in which every other house is a gas station or a sweetheart tearoom, and where there are richer politicians." It was his eloquence and persistence which had first persuaded the voters to amend the Protective By-Laws of Duxbury, increasing the minimum lot frontage of a hundred feet to a hundred-and-fifty, and the lot area of twenty thousand square feet to thirty thousand. The controversy over this proposal was mild, relatively speaking, for no zoning debate is ever really mild. Then came the recommendation to further amend the town's zoning laws, to require lots of no less than forty thousand square feet, with a two-hundred-foot frontage.

For months preceding the town meeting at which this problem would be solved, the *Clipper* had hammered away at the theme that firmer zoning requirements were our only defense against unscrupulous developers whose "row" houses would hike the tax rate, as had happened in other towns. After extensive research, we gave data on towns which had awakened too late to their zoning needs, and, to bolster our argument, we published this letter received from the editor and president of *Banker & Tradesman:*

My attention has been called to your editorial, "Roads in New Developments," in your issue of December 13. I would like to compliment you on it. You have made two points very clear—that the welcome mat is out for all your new residents, and that those who bring these new residents in have an obligation to the town and its taxpayers in the matter of roads. I was glad to see you cite Natick, for I have been quite conversant with what has been done there and feel that a good example has been set. As to the editorial itself, it conforms to what I have always felt was the real job of an editor—to lead the thinking of his community always along constructive lines.

Our stand was backed by the Finance Committee, Planning Board, and Board of Selectmen, although it was not politically expedient at the time for the three town fathers to take sides openly on this burning issue, since feelings ran incredibly high.

The *Clipper* advisory board was also unanimously in favor of the new zoning proposal.

Although we had pointed out time and again that the change in the zoning bylaws was not designed to cause hardship to any groups—since Duxbury, with its almost twenty-five square miles, was still only sparsely settled and had an abundance of inexpensive, attractive land—a few citizens, fishing in troubled waters, charged that the *Clipper* was discriminating against the underpossessed. Counter to the usual *Clipper* policy of publishing dissenting points of view, we flatly refused to print one letter which, we felt, distorted facts and threw a pinch of dust into the eyes of truth. It was written by a local police officer who has since become a good friend of ours. When we returned the letter, he sent this open letter to all box-holders and R.F.D.'s:

I wrote the following letter to the editor of a local Duxbury newspaper, to be published. This letter was written BEFORE THE PUBLIC HEARING. The editor has not seen fit to publish it.

LETTER TO THE EDITOR

You may put me down as one who is opposed to the proposed increase of lot sizes to forty thousand square feet.

I think the people backing this Article are unaware of, or just do not care about the younger generation who are here, or those who are coming along who would like to build their homes here in Duxbury. Every time lot sizes are increased they are also increased a very sizeable amount of money in price, and all people are not born "well to do."

Times are getting tough enough without home owners who are secure financially making it still harder for others to get started. Look at your own house and land and at about ninety per cent of the properties on Washington Street and in the village area and see how many could qualify under the zoning laws and proposed building code that you are trying to push onto the lowly unfortunates.

If you really believe that the town needs this excessive zoning protection, how come that you and the others are satisfied with what you have?

I say, zone the town into areas according to population and then zone the areas into house lots after a thorough consideration of what is best for that location. Like you are proposing to do at Duxbury Beach.

When the writer of this letter, which was certainly not without merit, refused to delete the statement about the *Clipper*'s trying to push zoning laws and a building code "onto the lowly unfortunates," we rejected it, since we felt these inflammatory words distorted facts. The writer of the letter realized this later himself. Today he is proud of his hundred acres of land in an attractive part of Duxbury, and will admit that he does not qualify for the description of "lowly unfortunate."

The police officer also erred when he said those of us with small plots of land and limited frontage were "satisfied." Bobbie and I, like many other residents of the "village," feel somewhat cramped with our hundred-foot frontage. A neighboring house is less than fifteen feet from ours. Current land owners, moreover, would not be in any way penalized, since no changes would be made in the status of registered plots.

The new zoning regulations (along with the building code adopted soon after) was good for the swarm, therefore good for the bee. If the *Clipper*'s motive had been selfish, it would have strenuously fought against the proposed changes, for the *Clipper* would have prospered if hundreds of "row" houses had been built, bringing in their wake supermarkets and other business enterprises which would have swelled advertising revenue.

Duxbury is full of residents who came or remained because they prefer horizontal living in a rustic setting; they did not buy homes with the idea of having their community turn into a congested settlement of "row" houses. With the scarcity of industry, how could the town afford such a crowded community that would, to cite one need, require so many new schools? Our thesis was backed by many working men as well as by the "well to do."

At one of the most crowded town meetings in Duxbury's history, and after debate that ranged from the spirited to the acrimonious, the vote was 345 to 152 in favor of the proposed zoning laws.

Since March of 1954, tempers have cooled, but after this meeting the air hung heavy with resentment. The police chief at the meeting had accused the *Clipper* of failing to present the opposite point of view, and we did not arise to defend our position, feeling the "opposition" had had its chance to express its point of view in "Sounding Off" (with the exception noted). The bitterness that usually evaporates at the end of town meeting, when "enemies" smile at one another and shake hands, was missing, and that night, as we learned later, protest meetings were held in various parts of town. There were dramatic consequences.

The protest groups, planning counter-action, were sure they could overthrow the new zoning regulations at the next annual town meeting. They enlisted the support of a beloved town character, who, many years earlier, had run a political machine in Duxbury and had virtually dictated who would be elected to public office, including the office of Selectman and Assessor. Call him Boss Skiffington, since that is not his name. The boss agreed the first move would be to depose the moderator who, according to the disgruntled, had not given the "anti-zoners" all the time they wanted to speak.

The distinguished moderator, forceful, high-minded and a gentleman of rugged principle, was a popular member of the community, although he had been a "year-rounder" only since 1941. "The job of the moderator," he told the *Clipper*, "is to get the town to state what it wants to do. It's almost as simple as that. As moderator, you've just got to take the position that good open discussion resolves any problem correctly almost always. You've just got to be objective and, without favoring one or another, arrive at decisions. The good old town meeting does a fine job of it."

The role of moderator is exacting, for there are always pressure groups to find fault if things don't turn out as they wish. If the Chief Justice of the Supreme Court presided at some town meetings, when there was a mood of revolt or bitterness, he even might be charged with being partial. Our moderator was clear-thinking and judicial in temperament, and he had a saving sense of humor. There were factions, nonetheless, who accused him of being arbitrary on occasion. One criticism leveled at him was that he addressed by their first names some townspeople who rose to speak, and asked other old-line residents to identify themselves. Since he was considered a newcomer, many oldtimers bridled when he did not appear to recognize them. He simply didn't know them.

When a moderator catches the mood of the assembly and notices the oratorical sails of windbags are luffing in the breeze, it is his duty, as well as prerogative, to cut off debate after a polite warning. Otherwise, the filibusters would have a field day. On this particular stormy Saturday afternoon an undercurrent of hostility clouded the central issue. At times it appeared that almost everyone wanted to speak at once. In the *Clipper's* opinion, the moderator did his best to recognize both pro and con speakers, some of whom weakened their arguments by faulty logic and a foolish display of temper. The climax speaker, many agreed later when the smoke of battle

184

cleared, was Tom Herrick, who was sitting in the balcony surrounded by a group who solidly opposed the zoning proposals. In a strong speech Tom said, in substance, that while he favored the zoning change, he would return to fight it the following year if he heard of any hardship that resulted from the change. His argument, well seasoned by salty whimsy, may have swung enough votes to put the amendment across. When he sat down, wild applause drowned out the boos, but there was a grim look on the faces of some of his friends in the balcony.

That night, when Tom threw his hat into Legion Hall, it came right back, as if on a reverse bounce. "I think I would have been mobbed if I had gone in at that time," he told us later. He was not, however, the only person who was non grata at the time. Among the villains of the coup, according to some of the more articulate opponents of the zoning change, were the *Clipper* editor and the moderator.

"Since there seemed to be no way we could get the *Clipper* editor," one "plotter" smilingly told us later—years later—"we decided to go after the moderator."

Duxbury, like most towns, has political cliques which thrive on behind-the-scene maneuvering. One group was well enough organized to determine the outcome of any school committee election. Taking advantage of the town's apathy in school matters, this clique hand-picked candidates. One night we "crashed" one of its back-stage conclaves, noticed that about forty persons were present. Most of them, we felt, were genuinely interested in electing able candidates, but we also noted a familiar "hard core" who used such groups as a part of a larger plan to run all elections.

When various names were suggested, an informal vote was taken. No single candidate received more than six votes. Yet the candidate of this unrepresentative group would virtually be assured of election!

After voicing our disgust, we headed for the rear entrance, figuring there were fewer obstacles in the line of retreat. The "organizer" collared us in the kitchen.

"I hope you're not going to mention these proceedings in the *Clipper*," he said.

"Not unless you decide on any of the candidates who were mentioned at your meeting," I said. "When forty persons can't agree on a suitable candidate, maybe you should make membership in your club more exclusive."

This group later agreed on a candidate of unquestionable ability. Since then, this particular clique has disbanded. There is no longer any political machine in Duxbury that can swing an election. Only a surprise move, carefully organized, can achieve that. "Boss Skiffington" proved that a few years ago.

Duxbury's town elections are held on the Saturday following the annual town meeting. The boss and his followers persuaded an able and distinguished citizen to run against the incumbent moderator on "stickers." All this was done in the approved cloak-and-dagger manner, and the secret was so well guarded, the *Clipper* did not learn of it in time to report it factually in the Thursday issue—two days before election. It is routine *Clipper* policy to list all candidates—including any who run on stickers.

It had taken a great deal of persuasion to get Mr. X to run against the incumbent, of whom he was and is fond. When, two days before the election, he asked what we thought of his running, we said he had a perfect right to run, that we were sure he would make a fine moderator, and that as far as the *Clipper* was concerned, he could count only on factual reporting. There would be no criticism or snide asides, overt or veiled.

"But we'll do everything possible personally to defeat you," we added. "We feel that our current moderator has done a good job." During our friendly chat, there was no doubt in our mind of his sincere reluctance to run under the circumstances, but the pressure put on him was terrific. It may be said to his credit that he told the incumbent of his intention to run, and that he would withdraw if the incumbent so advised. This the moderator refused to do.

The "opposition" had had almost a full week's head start when the pro-incumbent forces swung into action. It was not until after nine o'clock on the eve of the election that we launched our telephone campaign.

"I thought you said the *Clipper* would not take sides in political issues," remarked one of the people we called.

"The *Clipper* does not," we said. "This is John Cutler calling, not *The Duxbury Clipper*."

The "buttonholing" continued all during election day, but as the afternoon waned, we knew we were beaten. The issue was decided when a "political leader" who controlled almost two hundred votes switched his allegiance after telling us he was on our side. Mr. X won by a substantial margin. In the next issue of the *Clipper*, we reported what happened on election night:

Running on stickers, Mr. X was elected town moderator Saturday, a post his father held for eighteen years. The new moderator, unaware of the campaign in his behalf until last week, faces a difficult assignment. All who know him endorse him as an outstanding citizen and have every confidence that he will do his utmost to perform the exacting duties of his office. We congratulate him and wish him every success.

His predecessor handed over the gavel to him in a spirit of cooperation that is characteristic of the high-minded person he is. At 7:25 P.M., shortly before the polls closed, the incumbent went to Mr. X's house and asked him to come down to the election meeting in the interests of harmony. There were about fifty persons present when the incumbent walked to the podium and announced that the election results were 530 to 381 in favor of Mr. X.

He then recalled the occasion when his predecessor came to him, said he was resigning and suggested that the incumbent be a candidate for the office. The incumbent told all present how much he appreciated the honor and trust accorded him by the town, adding: "I have tried to be impartial and fair these six years as moderator, but apparently my services were displeasing in some respects. I am delighted at this time to present your new moderator and to assure you that I shall give him my support and cooperation."

After accepting the gavel, Mr. X said: "The citizens of Duxbury have bestowed on me a very great honor and trust. The very same honor and trust that were bestowed on you, and which you have so ably borne these past six years. I will try to do as well as my predecessor."

Here was a touching little drama that left some of those present misty-eyed.

Incidents that followed were not on such a high plane. Two men on election night, obviously in their cups, phoned the incumbent and tried to heckle him—most unsuccessfully. "I didn't realize what a nice guy he was," one said later. "He was such a good sport about the way I kidded him, he made me feel like a heel."

That was the *Clipper*'s first real baptism of fire, and it was long in coming. For months we were more conscious than usual of glares. There were a frosty few who drove past us without the customary friendly wave, the small-town salute. But the day came when one of the Selectmen said: "Even some of the most bitter critics now realize our zoning regulations have saved the town. They now know that Duxbury will grow, but not explosively."

It was months before we learned of the role played by

188

"Boss Skiffington." We asked a veteran town official, by this time retired, how the "sticker" election had been planned.

He grinned owlishly. "Well, for a good many years, now, Skiffington left his steam roller rusting on the side of the road. Then one day he oiled it up and put it to work. Now it's back there rusting, again, but you never know. . . ."

Hearing that Skiffington was counting on using his "steam roller" to reinstate the old zoning law at the next annual town meeting, we assured him we would acquaint the townspeople of any back-stage maneuvering the next time out. He said he had no intention of moving his steam roller out again, and he never has.

The selection of candidates for elected office should not be engineered by pressure groups or weekly newspapers. A weekly that tries to dictate elections would soon lose the respect of its readers. It is the function of the editor merely to point out, enlighten, clarify.

Considering the heavy seas that have buffeted the *Clipper* during the past decade, it was with surprise and satisfaction that we received this letter from the chairman of the Board of Selectmen soon after the zoning squall:

At this time the Selectmen would like to thank you for your efforts to inform the townspeople concerning all the details involved if the town and the district vote that the town shall absorb the district.

We appreciate your taking the time and making the effort to acquaint yourself with the many ramifications resulting from the votes passed at the 1955 annual town meeting.

Then, after correcting an error we made, he added:

Your public spirited efforts are far too valuable to be criticized because of one minor error, and we have written you only because we believe you are sincerely interested in giving the voters a complete and truthful picture of the results of their votes. . . . We have been remiss on many occasions in failing to express our deep gratitude for the fine work you and your paper have done. The *Clipper*, so doubtfully received a few years ago, has won its place in town affairs and serves to educate the voter and assists in bringing about a keener interest in every municipal problem.

Did we publish this nice letter in the *Clipper*? Yes, indeed!

CHAPTER 17

"Doing business without advertising is like winking at a girl in the dark. You know what you are doing, but nobody else does."

—PUBLISHERS' AUXILIARY

A survey made recently by Brigham Young University revealed that weekly newspapers have a whopping ninety to a hundred per cent readership, while daily newspapers have only thirty-four per cent. Radio and television? According to the survey, radio has a fourteen per cent listening—TV the same per cent viewing—audience.

Other studies have shown that a weekly, instead of being hastily scanned and discarded, is more closely read by more members of the family. The adage—"There is nothing older than yesterday's newspaper"—does not always apply to a properly run weekly. "We doubted, too, that the weekly stays 'live' in the home for a week," a reader wrote in *The Publishers' Auxiliary*. "We advertised for a metronome, let the ad run five times: no results, except a few calls to find out what in the heck a metronome was. We pulled the ad, and six weeks later got a call from a lady who had one. She had seen the ad in a paper at a friend's home. Not one week, but at least six weeks."

If a weekly carries only items of ephemeral interest it will soon find its way to the wastebasket, of course, but the paper that contains articles of lasting interest may be kept for a long time. This is not the only feature of weeklies that interests advertisers.

"No combinations of media published and circulated nationally can stand up against the local newspapers of a community in any comparison of thorough market coverage through net paid reader circulation." That statement appears in the brochure, "Establishing and Operating a Weekly Newspaper."

"Nor can editorial content of national interest compare with local news as a background helpful toward getting the advertiser's message read," the brochure adds.

More and more, the weekly paper is attracting advertisers who see its sales appeal as a good investment, for it reaches the public they wish to sell. "The suburban weekly," according to the government brochure, "has become an important element in merchandising goods on the one hand, and a highly specialized community force on the other." And why not, mates? Isn't ALL business eventually local?

When a new weekly suddenly appears in a community unused to such an interloper, it may, as was *The Duxbury Clipper*, be "doubtfully received." Local merchants may insert an ad to help it get going or adopt a wait-and-see policy. They have to be sold not only on the effectiveness of a weekly in peddling their services or products, but also on the proven axiom that best results are obtained from constant, rather than from sporadic, advertising.

The manager of a nearby drive-in theater was dubious about continuing his regular weekly ad in the *Clipper* until an error appeared in the chronological listing of a feature film. When drivers honked angrily because the show did not start "on schedule," the manager explained that they were an hour too early.

"Then why in hell did you put the wrong time in *The Dux-bury Clipper?*" one patron said. The manager was suddenly convinced that his ads were being read.

Prospective advertisers sometimes discover the "pull" of a weekly by accident. A newspaper strike in Boston a few years ago brought this comment from the president of the Boston Real Estate Board, and be sure that the *Clipper* was among the South Shore weeklies that printed it:

The value of the local home town weekly newspaper was dramatically highlighted by the Boston newspaper strike. Our realtor members found out more than ever before how valuable the advertising columns of their local home town papers were in selling houses or in renting apartments. This holds true in all other lines of business, for while local weeklies do not offer the widespread coverage and mass circulation of a metropolitan daily or Sunday newspaper, they are most effective in their own areas and give near saturation coverage of their local communities. They also get a high degree of reader interest into their columns, and this, of course, benefits advertisers. This stems from their strong news coverage of local people and events. Everyone in a small town wants to know what his neighbors are doing.

Local display advertising is generally considered to be a weekly publisher's most fruitful source of revenue. This income, especially in recent years, is supplemented by national advertising, since manufacturers' budgets allocate a share of the national money to appliance or automobile dealers in the communities. It is the practice of most weeklies, since their publishers must pay an agency commission, to charge higher rates for national display advertising to compensate for the commission charges.

Since advertising revenue pays most of the freight, the weekly editor should help his clients write colorful copy to give their messages more pulling power. Once customers have confidence in you, they will say, "Set it up the way you think best."

Don't hesitate, on the other hand, to use a "tease-the-sponsor" approach. The *Clipper* regularly uses fillers designed to encourage advertisers to part with money. Samples:

"There is one place where money is made without advertising, and that's the Mint."

"When a businessman said he was cutting his advertising outlay to save money, an advertising salesman asked him why he didn't stop his watch and save time."

Local advertisers deserve an occasional plug. Once in a while remind readers that the town merchants, nice people, welcome your patronage.

We hope you enjoy reading *The Duxbury Clipper* each week before using it to wrap around potted plants. If you do like our little sheet, show your appreciation by patronizing the local advertisers who help bring it to you each week. Although the number of out-of-town paid subscriptions is growing, it has not yet surpassed the circulation of *The New York Times*; and if we had to depend on that source of revenue we'd have to revert to the habit of eating warmed-over peanuts. The advertisers who help bring you the *Clipper* each week don't like warmed-over peanuts, either. They expect their ads to pull. Let's patronize our local advertisers, hey?

We might add that our local merchants are repeatedly called upon to donate goods or services to auctions, fairs, church suppers—to practically everything from a quilting bee to a strawberry festival. They indirectly send Duxbury youngsters to camp; they donate the food that makes those Tarkiln Recreation camp suppers so reasonable, yet profitable.

"I admit I'm a clutchpenny," the oldtimer says, "but I believe in patronizin' local merchants. I even buy my cut plug down the center now, instead of growin' my own."

Other revenue comes from the publication of "legals"—official notices, proceedings of local appeal boards, proposals

194

for bids on equipment to be purchased by the town, and notices of foreclosures and special town meetings, along with those of Sheriff's sales and Probate and Land Court notices. Legals constitute profitable business for a weekly, for they are paid for at higher rates, since legals must be printed with the utmost accuracy.

"Legal notices are usually awarded to the paper located in the county seat," says the government brochure. This is not always true. The *Clipper*, which is not located in the county seat, receives many legals.

Another lucrative field—one often neglected by country editors—is classified advertising. Classifieds range from offers of jobs and real estate to the sale of roller skates, bicycles, tractors and automobiles, along with the "losts" and "founds."

"You can make these ads more effective by classifying them carefully," says the government brochure. Nonsense! The more you mix them up, the more they will be read. Week in and out, *Clipper* classifieds, except for social items in "Around Town," are the most closely read items in the paper.

The country editor can make "classifieds" more effective and readable by injecting a light touch. Samples:

FOR SALE: Duxbury duck in race-winning condition, but hurry, HURRY. Call WE 4-2811 after 5 A.M.

HELP! HELP! Business is simply awful, and we are just a couple of prep schoolers trying to turn an honest dollar. Saunter down to THE SNACK BAR. Sorry, no warm cokes.

WANT TO RELAX at your own party? Call Carol Holcombe or Beebles Lawson and ignore the wants of your guests.

HAVE LAWN MOWER, will travel. Lawn manicuring a specialty, and our touch is loving.

USED SCREENS still capable of frustrating gnats and mosquitoes. Back up your Cadillac and take them away for a pittance.

195

When we inserted the last ad on used screens we received more than thirty phone calls.

In one "classified," we made an error in the sale price of a beach buggy, offering it with "new brake linings" for fifteen dollars (instead of seventy-five). The person who inserted the ad was swamped with telephone calls. P.S. He got his price.

Hundreds of *Clipper* advertisers have told us of good results received from their classifieds. "I always succeed in getting whatever I advertise for in the *Clipper*," one resident said. "I was looking for a baby sitter," another wrote. "I got one, but I also wound up buying a swimming pool." Another comment: "Your classifieds are so interesting. Almost as good as *True Confessions*." We often receive such brief notes as: "My deepfreeze was sold by noon Thursday. Thanks."

You have established another paying precedent. Soon others are tossing posies at your "classifieds." One resident, giving himself a free "plug," wrote in "Sounding Off": "I have had 367% profit on my *Clipper* ads." Others got into the act: "I cannot speak too strongly of the power of your want ads," said the author of the *Clipper*'s garden column. "Note the attached envelope addressed to 'Mr. Peat Moss, Duxbury.' It reached me at once."

Display advertisers joined the chorus: "Two weeks ago," a local naval architect and boat broker wrote in "Sounding Off," "this firm advertised a 168-foot Twin Screw Diesel yacht in *The Duxbury Clipper*. We have advertised the subject vessel through no other medium than the *Clipper*, and yet, by this weekend, we received an inquiry from a South American client expressing interest in a yacht of this size and in her price range. This is indeed an outstanding example of the circulation encompassed by your paper and of the tremendous value afforded to your advertisers."

Even if this was a tongue-in-cheek observation, it was no less effective.

One of our original advertisers, Jackson Kent, has never missed placing an ad since the first issue, "with no harmful results that are perceptible," he says. One of his notes which helped his business as much as ours: "I'd like to report good results from my *Clipper* ads on GRIP, the no-slip, no-mess neck-saver for walks, steps and driveways. Good *Clipper* readers from Wellesley, Boston and Needham placed orders by phone and post card."

Since it was all in good fun, a crass commercial note might even creep into the "Around Town" column: "A classified ad found John Morton's beagle," was one "social" item. "Does this mean the beagle can read?" We further noted that while Stephen Rich sold his bicycle an hour after the *Clipper* came out on Thursday, it took Bobbie Mullowney an hour and ten minutes to sell hers.

And so it went. Residents found an easy way to sell pianos, trumpets, stoves, skis, sausages, lamps, and ice skates.

CLASSIFIED ADS BRING RESULTS

Look in your attic; you may find a scooter or umbrella you don't want which someone may need. You may even find a pair of galoshes someone left the last time they visited you.

That is a little "box" we occasionally run in the paper.

The growth of the classified ad column is a definite index of the popularity of your weekly. When one reader tells another that a dollar ad sold a used tractor, it gives the second fellow an idea. He may think of that extra lawn mower he doesn't use and would like to sell.

Circulation revenue for *The Duxbury Clipper* comes only from "out-of-towners," since the paper is still delivered free to all Duxbury families. This income ($4.50 per annum, $3.50 for nine months, 50¢ a month) pays part of the cost of production. (These rates were halved during the Korean conflict for all servicemen who received the *Clipper* as a gift from the local post of the American Legion.)

Here, again, there are ways of hiking paid circulation figures. Many parents entered subscriptions for children away at school when we published these words of a professor of journalism at the University of Utah:

Students away from home are happier, do better work and get better grades when they receive news from home. A subscription to the local newspapers for the serviceman or student will do wonders for his morale and effectiveness.

A free lecture of this sort should be fortified with such teasers as:

EDITOR, DUXBURY CLIPPER:

Can you please explain what "de rigueur" means and illustrate its use in a sentence?

JUST CURIOUS

("*De rigueur*" is a French phrase meaning "obligatory for good form." Example: "Duxbury parents with children away at school consider it *de rigueur* to send them *The Duxbury Clipper*. A few heartless parents disagree. —Ed.)

Use further reminders as space fillers. Just before one Christmas this item appeared in "Around Town":

According to the December issue of *Good Housekeeping*, a good Christmas present for a college boy is "a subscription to his home-town newspaper." This periodical suggests this as a gift "nobody else may have thought of," in which category it includes a good paperweight (such as an old brass doorknob, mounted) "for a casual beau or man friend."

It is safe to say there is one gift a college boy would prefer to a subscription to his local newspaper—a monogrammed checkbook, with Dad's autograph on the lower right corner of each check.

Periodically we list new *Clipper* passengers, including those attending boarding school, and this usually brings in more subscriptions. Insert a convenient subscription blank now and then, and remind readers that a subscription is a gift that keeps on giving.

"We have a few *Clipper* subscriptions left if you insist on giving a friend a surprise anniversary present," we wrote in one issue. "There is no truth to the rumor that there are no other subscriptions available, but you better act fast before we lift the gangplank."

Although our subscription list is not imposing, it is select, for many of the readers are writers, artists, professors, and historians. Today the *Clipper* is mailed to more than half of the States in the Union (including Alaska and Hawaii), and to England, Belgium and Switzerland, as well as to a dozen military posts scattered over the globe.

The country editor, to stimulate the tendency to subscribe may write himself a letter:

You say six or seven recalcitrant mossbacks who read the *Clipper* at no cost during the summer do not subscribe to it in the winter? Don't these pinch-pennies realize that the winter information is of interest to them tax-wise as well as otherwise? Don't they care about what cruises their friends are taking while they keep their noses to the grindstone? Is it because they fear they might be considered status seekers that they dare not enter a subscription? Please publish their names in your next issue and I shall be happy to send these pikers the *Clipper*.

$UCCE$$FUL WOOL MERCHANT

(What? Publish their names and expose them for what they are? —Ed.)

Some of your subscribers, Mr. Weekly Publisher, may need to be reminded that their subscription has run out. Why tell them so bluntly? Instead, publish one of the several letters you will receive. Here is one that just came in the mail: "Enclosed my check for another year's cruise aboard the *Clipper*. I can think of no happier check to write than this one." Another that comes to mind: "I enclose my check for $4.50 for one year's subscription to your excellent publication. The *Clipper* is read by every member of my family, a reader interest which is not attained by some of your competitors such as the Boston *Herald*, *Time* Magazine, *Reader's Digest*, or *Yachting*. Could you give me some idea of your circulation?"

(Certainly. Circulation of the *Clipper*, as compared with that of *Life* Magazine and *The New York Times*, is: (1) *Life*; (2) *New York Times*; (3) *Duxbury Clipper*. —Ed.)

So there you are, shipmates. If you toot your trumpet enough, the tendency may become contagious. We received one letter with this opening salutation: "Dear Best Paper on the South Shore." We never complained because Herman Smith gave the *Clipper* a plug when he was a guest on a radio program in Boston or because the *Clipper* received a favorable notice on the New England Almanac morning program (WEEI), when excerpts from an article we wrote on a basement museum in Plymouth were read and referred to as "valuable contributions to Americana."

And when we were interviewed on a TV program in Provi-

dence, Rhode Island, what could we say when asked if the *Clipper* was popular? "Why, yes, come to think. Now that you ask, I guess so. . . ."

Bobbie deserves most of the credit for the *Clipper's* booming volume of advertising, for she has patience, tact, and a warm understanding of human nature that her husband possesses to an alarmingly lesser degree. In days when the *Clipper* solicited advertising (it just comes, now), Bobbie was in complete charge of the program.

Was she ever scandalously negligent of her duties? Never! Once, however, she let me fill in as advertising executive. Let her tell the story:

One week John had less help from me than usual, but there was nothing I could do about it, for it's difficult to time the birth of a child.

When I awoke on Monday morning, I knew it was the day for the arrival of our fifth offspring. After getting my things together and putting the living room in order, I cooked breakfast for the children, woke John, and told him the news.

"You'll have to get the ads this morning," I said. This meant he would have a rough time getting the copy together, but I knew he could manage.

After telling the children they would have a new brother or sister when they returned from school, I called my doctor, who was in the shower, said his wife. When I told her I had to get over to Jordan Hospital in Plymouth quickly, she brought word from the doctor for us to hurry and he would follow as fast as he could.

Speeding over icy roads, we almost skidded into one slow driver, who was all over the road. The doctor passed us just as we were pulling into the hospital driveway. We rushed in, and John pressed the elevator button.

"I can't wait for the elevator," I said, hurrying up the stairs to the appropriate room.

"There's no mad rush," the doctor said after examining me. "I'll be back after I have a cup of coffee." He paused at the door. "I'll tell John he might as well go along, since it may be some time yet."

Five minutes later, with the doctor back just in time, John Ricketts Cutler was born. Although I wanted to call John right away at the Plymouth County Electric Company or Puritan Clothing Company—his first two stops for ads—the nurse made me lie still for another ten minutes. By the time I had called the electric company, John had left. Almost an hour later I reached him at home. He was surprised to hear from me so soon. Yes, he said, he had picked up all the Plymouth and Kingston ads.

"I didn't call about that," I said. "It's a handsome boy. Dr. Deacon thinks he looks like you and the nurse thinks he is more like Robert, but I think he looks like David." I stopped talking when I realized he had hung up. Worried? Oh, no. He never faints. I knew he couldn't wait to see his new son.

That was such a peaceful week, since having a baby gives a mother of four young children—pardon, five—such a wonderful rest. John brought over several books and magazines, along with yarn for knitting and my mother's FM radio. I felt a little guilty, just lying there being waited on and eating delicious meals. Now and then I glanced out the window at the teal-blue look the ocean always has in January, and I could see the snow-covered sandspit across the bay.

Suddenly I realized it was the end of the month. I told John to bring over the adding machine, bill heads, ruler, pen and complete copies of the December *Clippers*. I had to get the bills out so money would come in, since babies, unlike *Clippers*, are not delivered free.

I did the bookkeeping on the sliding table which hospitals provide for food trays and wash basins. The only interruptions were soothing back-rubs by the nurse, visits, food trays and fleeting glimpses of the future Little League All-Star. For once the bills were in the mail early. Normally, it's much more of a struggle to do the bookkeeping, along with getting ads, answering the phone and keeping the house shipshape.

It was back to the grind for me after six days. In my absence, the twins, then almost twelve, had vacuumed the rugs and arranged flowers around the house in appropriate containers. Jean Stetson had sterilized bottles and had a neat crib ready, while Betty Hutton fixed a meat loaf and baked an apple pie for our Sunday dinner. It was grand to be home feeling so rested. The whole thing was over, and the timing couldn't have been better. Tomorrow would be the start of another *Clipper* week, and although I was not quite ready to make the advertising rounds, I could at least handle some of the telephone calls while taking care of Ricky.

Now Ricky is old enough to handle some of those phone calls himself.

CHAPTER 18

"Look, son, do you have rocks in your head? A weekly newspaper would never click in little old Duxbury. There just plain isn't enough news."

—A Long-Time Resident

The average person in Duxbury in 1950 would have agreed that there was not enough news to support a weekly, and the early *Clippers* supported these contentions. It was not until the paper reported the underbrush escapades of the Peeping Tom that the *Clipper* carried its first sensational story. The head on the lead story was a daring departure from its sedate predecessors:

SHOTGUN USED TO
ROUT PEEPING TOM

In the following issue the head was:

NO CLUE TO PEEPING TOM
WHO TWICE RETURNS

By this time residents of the wooded sector off Washington Street were getting jittery, and the lovely housewife who had caught several glimpses of the peeper, was spending sleepless nights.

After being shot at on Monday night, he returned Friday, grinning foolishly through the kitchen window. He also came back shortly after dusk the following night, when Mr. X again fired at him, after snapping on the three floodlights he recently installed so he could have a better look at the prowler. Again the man disappeared into the pine woods off Huckleberry Lane. It was his sixth appearance—and disappearance—in nine days.

No, nothing ever happens in little old Duxbury. . . . What in the world do folks do in the winter?

One winter, John Parker and Roger Howland were transporting a heifer and a five-hundred-pound bull through the neighboring city of Providence when they stopped at a red light. The jarring stop frightened the bull so much, it lunged loose and plunged into down-town traffic. (Perhaps further infuriated by the sight of the red light?)

Parker whipped a rope out of the truck and like a seasoned cow-poke tried to lasso the charging bull. He made it on the sixth twirl of the improvised lariat. Then the problem: how do you hoist five hundred pounds of roughloin on the hoof onto a truck? A cinch. While onlookers rolled over the bull and held him down, John and Roger bound his legs and with the help of a few muscle men lifted it onto the truck.

Parker, who operates an express agency, said it was the most interesting package he ever delivered.

Duxbury and Providence were again cofeatured when Rusty, a mongrel (the *Clipper* misprint, "mangrel," almost got us in bad with a local member of the ASPCA), trotted fifty miles from Pawtucket, Rhode Island, to his Duxbury home.

"Rusty's exploit," we said, "is all the more astounding to anyone who has tried to thread his way through the maze of Providence's unmarked roadways without a compass. How Rusty managed to follow that Route 6 detour is incredible."

Our roving reporter had no trouble interviewing Penny Converse of Washington Street when she returned from Alaska, where she shot two Kodiak bears, but he got nowhere when he took a photographer to get a shot of a Duxbury resident on the day she became a centenarian. Although Abbie Litchfield turned a hundred years old on Thanksgiving, she felt she owed no gratitude to the two gentlemen from the *Clipper* (well, they used to call Boston *Transcript* reporters "gentlemen," didn't they?), and curtly told them to forthwith vacate the premises. Abbie had the kind of independence we hope to achieve by the time we're a hundred.

Small towns have moments of drama. *Clipper* readers were jolted to read this head:

T-MEN SMASH STILL ON MAYFLOWER STREET

Two officers from the Treasury Department, who hid in Duxbury for a week, smashed a still found in the woods near an old cellar hole.

The T-Men, who wore hunting clothes during the stake-out, had been watching the area since November 27, when they found the still in operation. They found 180 gallons of mash that would have produced thirty gallons of alcohol.

What, this in Duxbury???

To give the story a folksy touch, we added that a local game warden was suspicious of the "hunters'" antics until he saw their credentials.

Even in small towns, firemen carry trapped occupants of houses down ladders and the police may summon wreckers to fish an automobile that went through a bridge railing out of the bay. Two sensational stories involved sea tragedies which occurred a year apart to the day:

DID TRANI GO DOWN
IN THE DUXBURY SQUALL?

This referred to Richard Tingey, a nuclear power manager of Bethlehem Steel Shipbuilding Division, who sailed out of Quincy Bay in September of 1958 on his sloop, the Trani. He was off Duxbury on a Sunday when a vicious squall overturned his sloop. A lobster fisherman found his boat in fifty feet of water six days later off Powder Point Bridge. Tingey was directing construction of an atomic cruiser at the Fore River Shipyard.

A year later a Navy commander, who had left classified information in a parked car, also sailed through Duxbury waters. One evening the *Clipper* phone rang. A Duxbury teenager and a friend, while driving a beach buggy on Duxbury Beach, found the body at the highwater mark, with one leg missing. Some of the gruesome details recounted by the Duxbury youngster did not find space in the *Clipper*.

More palatable news was a reported wreck of an old Spanish galleon in the water off Brant Rock, a short distance from Duxbury Beach. Edward Rowe Snow of nearby Marshfield, an author known locally for his "Flying Santa Claus" exploits, and a Navy diver investigated the wreck and recovered pieces of eight, a large shield, cannon balls and a dagger. They also spotted what appeared to be a three-thousand-pound anchor near the wreck. The recovered coins bore dates in the 1600's.

A country weekly should always emphasize the local angle. When it was rumored that Robert Montgomery, the former Hollywood actor and White House assistant, might succeed Albert Pratt, a Duxbury property owner, as Assistant Secretary of the Navy, the *Clipper* accent was on Pratt, not Montgomery.

Clipper readers were interested to read that the former Barbara Thomas of Washington Street had been presented to the King and Queen of England at Buckingham Palace, but they were more impressed to hear what one resident told our *Clipper* reporter: "Why did I skip the Coronation? Helen and I had to rush home in time to see 'Duxbury Days.'" This gentleman never lets us know, on the other hand, when he is entertaining such celebrities as Roy Larsen or Curtis Roosevelt (formerly Curtis Dall), but we usually find out these things through one of our snoop-scoops.

There always seems to be some newsy little item to add sauce. When Mr. and Mrs. Gordon Couch appeared on Don McNeil's Breakfast Club show in Chicago, Don asked her name:

"Couch," she said.

"Davenport?" asked McNeil.

"No," she said, "Duxbury."

All right, *don't* laugh.

When nothing of any great moment is happening, there are local color items—the kind that occur in any town, Mr. Prospective Editor.

"Earl Russell's car was missing when he came out of The Village Pharmacy," we reported. "He cross-examined the proprietor and phoned the police. The trail led to the home of Betty Nickerson. Betty and her neighbor, Phyllis Conathan, were having a cup of coffee. What was Earl's car doing in front of the house?

"Seems that Phyllis, whose Mercury was a twin of Earl's car, had driven off in the wrong car! Charges were dropped."

Barbara Mallowney had taken a casserole to a sick friend when a stranger carrying a black bag knocked at the kitchen door.

"Nothing today," she said, "the lady of the house is ill, and—" Barbara was irked when he put his foot in the door.

"I'm *sorry*, but you simply can't come—" She headed for

the phone to call the police when the stranger pushed open the door and entered the kitchen. Barbara eyed the black bag.

"And she already has all the brushes she—"

"It's all right," he said. "Don't try to give me the brush. I'm Dr. Hamilton, her physician."

Every town has its vignettes, and you will flush them out if you let your readers know of your interest in them. Example:

While driving through Duxbury, two women, noticing an open door in an old house, peeked in and chatted with a man cleaning the ceiling. In answer to a query, he mentioned that he was president of Tufts University. Dr. H. C. Bumpus (whose son by the same name still lives in Duxbury) chuckled a moment later when he heard the women tell a friend who had stayed in the car: "There's an old coot in there who thinks he's president of Tufts." That's precisely who it was, mesdames.

Mrs. Michael Caliri, a former resident of Sudbury, Massachusetts, sold her house on Partridge Road, Duxbury, to Mrs. Kendall Way of Sudbury. She learned that the first name of the new resident was Nancy. Mrs. Caliri's maiden name? Nancy Way. We were beginning to wonder whether the road was becoming a One-Way street.

Life in Duxbury includes the story of a police alert at 1:40 A.M. In an emergency call, the operator reported that the telephone receiver was off the hook in the Robert Mullowney home, and a low moaning sound could be heard. The officer who rushed to the scene found Drummer, a Cocker puppy, woofing in her sleep.

The Richard Platts were watching television in their living room one night when a strange couple breezed in without knocking, poured themselves a cocktail, and sat down. "Can't I get you folks a drink?" the strange gentleman asked.

"No, thanks," Mr. Platt said.

"Well, let me see if I can find some crackers and cheese,

or something," the stranger said. He drained his drink and headed for the kitchen.

After some disjointed conversation, the stranger asked the Platts where they came from.

"Right here," Mrs. Platt said.

"Well, you certainly have a nice little old town. You live in a colonial, I suppose. Bill told me about your colonials."

"Well, this isn't exactly a colonial," Mr. Platt said.

"Hold the phone until I get another snort. How about you folks?"

"Who is the Bill you mentioned?" Mr. Platt said when the stranger returned from the kitchen.

"Bill Scherff. You know—the chap who owns this house. Maybe I better call up to him."

"I don't think Bill will be able to hear you," Mrs. Platt said. "You see, we bought this house from him a few months ago, and he now lives at the other end of town—in a colonial, I think."

When Neal O'Hara mentioned in his "Traveler" column that he knew of no golfer who had ever scored two holes-in-one on the same golf course, we sent him this *Clipper* newsclip: "William Fletcher of Bradford Road has scored three holes-in-one on the Duxbury Golf Course. One of his aces went in on the fly."

Even a cemetery in a small town may furnish copy, for sometimes the last words of the deceased pack a punch. In Mayflower Cemetery in Duxbury is this epitaph, cut on the tombstone of Asenath Soule, who died in 1865 at the age of eighty-seven: "The chisel can't help her any."

One story flushes out another, and a simple query may become a widening ripple. We received a note from a resident of Duxbury, Vermont, and a letter from the Reverend C. L.

Duxbury, pastor of the First Christian Church in Mankato, Minnesota:

Our son John Duxbury will celebrate his fourteenth birthday anniversary on April first. He has always been so proud of Duxbury, Massachusetts, and looks forward to the day when he can visit your town. He is interested in journalism and hopes to be a sports writer some day. We would appreciate it very much if you could find time to write him a short note for his birthday on the stationery of the Duxbury Clipper.

In our note we told John Duxbury that our daughter, Gail, was also born on the first of April.

A former Duxbury dentist, then serving with the United States Navy, told our readers of a chat he had had with the crew of the *Duxbury Bay*, a seaplane tender. Duxbury students in the sixth grade, who were studying the geography of the Near East, were delighted to receive letters from members of the crew while the *Duxbury Bay* was patroling the Persian Gulf. Post cards and photographs were enclosed in some of the letters.

Readers from all over the country send in quaint items in which Duxbury is mentioned. One newsclip, from the *Louisville Courier-Journal*, reported a house had just been built in Duxbury for the first time in two hundred years!

And the fact that it is a contemporary house has caused worlds of trouble. At first they couldn't get a permit for such a house and finally had to appear before a town meeting with their architect and contractor. There was so much interest in the outcome that citizens of Duxbury turned out in full force. There was argument back and forth and finally it was settled when a gentleman on the town board announced, "I suppose the houses originally built in Duxbury didn't meet the building code either, and they're still standing over three hundred years later."

Nevertheless, townspeople drive by and stare constantly at the house. It's in an area called Tinkertown.

The fact is that many new houses had been built every year in Duxbury which, at the time, had no building code. And it would take a four-alarm fire at the very least to make the citizens of Duxbury turn out in full force!

The *Chicago Daily Tribune* had an equally quaint picture of Duxbury, which it called, in January 1954, "the last outpost of Americanism." In his cozy piece, a staffer said the "city" fathers allowed no building of ranch houses, or so-called "modern homes" (you should see some of them, sir). "Everything must conform to the architecture which has prevailed in the New England town for generations.... No one ever locks a door in Duxbury."

(NOTE: Residents who leave on trips frequently ask the *Clipper* to keep mum until their return, fearful of having their locked domiciles broken into.)

What happens to a tiny community when a hundred thousand dollars suddenly pours into the pockets of its residents— all of it new money? The story of boom time in Duxbury in 1954 and 1955, when residents found gold—in the form of bay scallops—in their mud flats, gave the *Clipper* an exciting story that attracted national interest.

Duxbury shellfish is world-famed. At the turn of the century, Duxbury clams were mentioned in cookbooks, and only their Ipswich cousins deserved to be compared with them. Epicures in remote places used to send to Duxbury for seed clams. By 1914, however, the supply of Duxbury clams had dwindled, and diggers were lucky to get half a dozen buckets from the mud flats between tides. The town's clam garden, planted in 1914, revived the industry.

In 1936, its peak year of production, Duxbury Bay was tapped for one hundred and seventy-seven thousand bushels of clams that sold at one dollar and fifty cents a bushel. By 1950, the same area gave up only a hundred and seventy bushels, which went for as high as five dollars a bushel. The clamming industry faded because of a change in the configuration of the coastline, water pollution, decline in the growth of eel grass and as a result of such predators as crabs and snails.

Duxbury historians who have dug into the clam story say clam chowder originated in Duxbury. Ruth Alden Bass, an early settler, was walking along the beach looking for driftwood when she saw pigs rooting for clams and eating them with relish (not Worcestershire, of course). Later, when her family faced famine while scratching for a living from barren soil on a storm-swept coast, Ruth remembered those foraging pigs. She dug a basketful of clams, boiled them in milk and set the dish before her husband, who said she must have been touched in the head to think of serving such fare.

"Better to die of the eating than the starving," said Ruth. They ate and survived.

The scallop boom came during another decline in the clam industry.

One morning in 1955, Bob White put-putted out to the north end of Clark's Island and dropped the hook. Exactly fifty-five minutes later he returned with his quota of four bushels of bay scallops which a New Bedford dealer checked to make sure did not contain too many mussels (which, by the way, make tasty morsels) or too much seaweed.

Bob's brief expedition was eloquent proof of the sudden and joyful abundance of the prized bivalves on over three hundred acres of mud flats lining Duxbury harbor, all within easy reach of a long-handled rake.

On this particular December day, the price of a bushel of scallops in shell was $4.75, with higher prices in prospect because of the scarcity of scallops around the Cape, Martha's Vineyard and Nantucket. Bob White, his two brothers and their father—Captain Norman White of the Duxbury Yacht

Club, all descended from sea captains—could earn as much as $513 a week on a three-hour working day during the boom. It was like finding a cluster of gold nuggets in one pile.

The Scallop Rush gave the *Clipper* an exclusive story. It noted that the unexpected bonanza worked wonders in the boom-bust economy of a town whose population dwindles during the winter.

The six-month scallop season had opened on October first, when word got around town that there was "sea gold" out on the flats by Clark's Island (named for the first mate of the *Mayflower*, John Clark). Suddenly the mud flats were populated with shellfishermen.

Scallops were not new to Duxbury. Towards the end of the past century they were so plentiful they were used as fertilizer on Duxbury's inland farms. Oldtimers we interviewed recalled years when they went "guzzling," a term that refers to scooping scallops from mud flats of tidal inlets or guzzles. But few scallops had been found since the bitterly cold winter of 1934-35 when children skated out to the main channel of Clark's Island. It was not until 1953-54 that the scallop population was impressive.

The sudden abundance was ascribed to the progressive warming of ocean water which brought the scallops above the Cape. By mid-November of 1954, Duxbury had the biggest catch of bay scallops ever known north of Cape Cod. Meanwhile, down in the Greater New Bedford area, there was an abrupt scallop famine.

The fever rose slowly in Duxbury. Few thought local scallops would challenge the established supremacy of the market. They blinked when Duxbury became the scallop capital of New England.

Cape and New Bedford dealers flocked into town to buy every bushel Duxbury could produce. When the price rose

214

to almost five dollars a bushel, eighty-one-year-old Maurice Chandler of Washington Street shook his head. "To think," he said, "that back in 1895 I sold nine hundred big lobsters it took me a week to trap for six cents each."

By mid-December, more than 12,000 bushels had netted Duxbury residents about $50,000 in fresh currency, most of it going to those who needed it.

"This beats raising chickens," a farmer said. "You don't have to coop or feed scallops or worry about raccoons, and they sell for more a pound." Right. Shucked scallops were sold for one dollar and twenty-five cents a pound, and if you were as expert as Bob White's brother, Joel, you could shuck out a bushel in forty minutes.

Duxbury was unprepared for the boom. None of the stores had scallop rakes, and an investigation revealed there was no such thing as a standard scallop rake. Each community had its own peculiar way of capturing scallops, whether by dragging, dredging (pronounced "drudgin'" by old salts), scoop nets or rakes. Duxbury improvised its own rakes, which varied in width from seven inches to twenty. Hardware stores sold every last shovel, pitchfork and rake. Coke rakes, normally used to remove clinkers from furnaces, were easier to fashion into scallop snatchers than some of the others, but they still needed long handles. A merchant came up with the solution—closet poles.

"I sold more closet poles in one week than I ever had previously in two years," said Ben Goodrich, Jr.

Dick Prince did a flourishing business at the Duxbury Garage making rakes, which he sold for twelve dollars. Vernon Stewart interrupted a repair job on the town's modern steam roller to make the rakes, when Prince was unable to keep up with the demand. After all, Dick had to go scalloping, too!

Business boomed all over town. Never in an off season did

marine appliance stores have such a run on new and used boats, outboard motors, caulking cements, oars, anchors and life jackets. It was the same story in other stores, with a heavy sale of hip boots, oilskins, heavy shirts, and foul-weather gear. Stan Roberts, who had bought Shiff's Store, struggled to meet the demand for long underwear, and he advertised "Scalloper Mittens" in the *Clipper*. One afternoon when Stan was out scalloping, a friend in a nearby boat called over: "I tried to get a pair of those mittens you advertised, but you were closed yesterday. Don't you want any more business?"

"How about you?" Stan asked. "I asked you a week ago to fix the leak on my porch, and like the rest of the carpenters, you were out scalloping."

Automobile mechanics, insurance agents, lawyers, teachers, realtors, airline pilots, firemen and policemen, joined the low-tide scallop fleet. Some quit their jobs to earn twice as much money doing three times less work. In the display window of Carl Santheson's Snug Harbor Fish Market was the sign: OPEN AT HIGH TIDE.

Overhead? All you needed was a $2.50 commercial permit, four burlap bags, a rake and warm gear.

The *Clipper* was primarily interested in the boom's impact on the local economy (we were too lazy to go out with the fleet). What happened? For one shut-in, it meant a yearned-for television set. Persons who hadn't traded a car for years bought the latest models. They paid old bills. A carpenter, giving his physician one hundred and fifteen dollars in cash, said: "You know, Doc, you delivered my daughter just about three years ago; it's time I delivered payment."

Families paid their back taxes and water bills, caught up with mortgage payments and opened savings accounts for the first time since they were married. One family decorated its Christmas tree with scallop shells; others used crushed shells to make unique driveways. The names on the welfare roll dropped, and accounts receivable, including the *Clipper*'s, dwindled.

The busiest person in town was Henry McNeil, a former professional boxer who, in addition to his duties as shellfish constable, was the town's burial agent and director of veterans' services. He was also a member of the police and fire departments and chief registrar for the draft.

One blustery November morning, several scallopers almost drowned when a squall hit a fleet of seventy small boats, swamping and capsizing some, sinking others. Three men were taken ashore exhausted after clinging to their capsized boat for an hour. One man lost eight bushels of scallops when his boat went down, and Henry McNeil caught up with three youngsters as their tiny craft, weighted with scallops, was shipping water.

Duxbury shellfishermen, unaccustomed to scalloping, knew little about shucking the bivalves, never having seen them in such commercial quantities. Most of them, therefore, shipped the scallops to New Bedford to be shucked, a job requiring considerable skill.

One resident who did his own shucking was Daniel Winsor, proprietor of the Winsor House, a charming inn with the appointments of a refined English pub. The Winsor House, a landmark since 1800, has a warm, friendly and dignified atmosphere. Its ancient pine-paneled, heavy-timbered dining room with its hand-hewn beams—its taproom with its Currier & Ives prints, open fireplace, candle sconces and massive tavern tables—make it unique. Dan Winsor, who is descended from a long line of sea captains who brought in cargo from China and the South Seas, raked in scallops, shucked them and served them to his guests. From mud flat to dinner plate—a good example of vertical combination.

Meanwhile, *The Duxbury Clipper*, in its description of the short, unhappy life of the scallop, warned local shellfishermen not to be too optimistic:

If we have a severe winter with anchor frost like the one in 1934-35, expect few scallops next year. Among the deadly enemies of the scallop are oyster drills, starfish, ducks that gobble up spat, and parasites that bind adult scallop shells. Barring a bitter winter, and unless high winds strip seedling scallops from their stones, shell and eel grass moorings, more money may flow into the till next year.

After one more prosperous year, the restless scallop revisited former haunts, and the shellfishermen of Duxbury went back to more prosaic pursuits.

Current news vies with news of Duxbury's past in the *Clipper*. In a nautical town, even non-nauts like to hear of Duxbury's seafaring days. In seeking such information we can always rely on Gershom Bradford, who has a passionate interest in truthful detail. When we inquired about the schooner *Duxbury*, mentioned in a short story in the Saturday Evening Post, he gave the history of the vessel, adding it had no connection with our town:

Another tantalizing historical point of local interest is why that dangerous reef in the northern approach of San Francisco Bay is charted as Duxbury Reef. There was a ship named *Duxbury* advertised as sailing from California in the gold rush days. As most reefs in the world have taken their names from ships that have come to grief on them, there is a possibility that the *Duxbury* may have been wrecked on that reef.

While almost every town has its ancient landmarks which its fathers have set, Duxbury, because of its age and connection with the Pilgrim story, has more than the average quota of shrines and historical associations. Here there is unmined romance and legend which no boilerplate can match.

When a reader asked what happened to the original *May-flower*, we dug into the files and discovered that after this vessel was broken up and sold for salvage in 1624, its seasoned oak timbers, bought by a Buckinghamshire farmer for a song, were used for the framework of his barn on an English country-side.

Another query: What happened to Duxbury Hall, the home of the ancestors of Captain Myles Standish? Here the *Clipper* got a beat, after a letter addressed to "His Worship, The Mayor, Duxbury, Mass., U.S.A.," was delivered to Philip Delano, chairman of the Board of Selectmen. We published the letter:

My Dear Mayor: I am enclosing a clip from the *Chorley Guardian* which gives a description of Duxbury Hall and a brief history of the hall and its occupants of bygone days. I know you of Duxbury, Massachusetts, will be particularly interested, since the illustrious and great leader, Myles Standish of Pilgrim Father fame, had close associations with this particular hall.

We were reading *The Strange Case of Alger Hiss* (by the Earl of Jowitt) when this item caught our eye: "Alger Hiss was born in November, 1904, at Baltimore. He was educated at the grammar school and high school there, from whence he went for a couple of terms to a prep school at Duxbury."

Research revealed that Hiss attended the old Powder Point School, located on the present site of the National Sailors' Home. In 1920-21, he lived in Grove House dormitory, a square colonial on the village green. We interviewed Henry Hurd of Duxbury, who lived with Hiss in Grove House:

He was a top student. He belonged to the T-Club, chemistry and dramatic clubs, and was an outstanding debater, I remember. Too slight to play football, he managed the team. The school we attended was used as a hotel during the summer.

Powder Point School had been brought to the attention of Hiss by his sister, a resident of Cambridge, Massachusetts, who became a year-rounder in the 1920's. A gracious person remembered for her charm and beauty, she took her own life in 1929 at the age of thirty-three. She died in a Plymouth hospital and was buried in Mt. Auburn Cemetery in Cambridge.

Much of Duxbury's fascinating history is little known. More than a century before the Brook Farm experiment, communism was tried in a section of town called Ashdod, where tall bushes still fringe a brook, and where red foxes are occasionally seen. Two Duxbury youths and their wives pooled their resources in a cooperative ownership and sparked a movement still remembered as the "Ashdod Brook Farm Experiment."

The old Ford Store, one of Duxbury's shrines, made headlines in Boston newspapers when it burned down in 1921. Oldtimers have recalled for *Clipper* readers some of the noted who patronized "America's first department store," including Adelaide Phillips, the world-famed contralto whose home was not far from Daniel Webster's in nearby Marshfield. (There is a marble statue of her on the lawn adjoining the house she lived in.) Here's a local anecdote about Dan Webster (Ford's Store is the scene):

"Take a hold, Mr. Webster, give us a lift, will ye?"

"Certainly." Daniel Webster tilted his high beaver hat on his leonine head and helped the storekeeper hoist a box of Havana sugar into the store.

The long rambling store had been established in 1779. Since the first railroad did not reach Duxbury until 1873, the old store used to have its goods brought by packet ship to Duxbury Beach, then transported about a mile to the store. Stagecoaches also delivered supplies to Ford's over the road from Boston, stopping at the original toll house, reception lounge of the present storied Toll House. Built in 1709 halfway between Boston and New Bedford, it was a toll house for travelers—a control point on a toll road. For generations it was a stopping place for seafarers and stagecoach passengers who dined while toll was paid and horses changed. Then, used as a home for 150 years, it was reopened in 1930 by the Kenneth Wakefields of Duxbury. Toll House has been host to Lady Astor, who gushed over its food; to Duncan Hines, who said: "Toll House is the kind of place that makes a fellow wish he had hollow legs," and to other celebrities.

Dan Webster, who lived less than two miles away in Marshfield, spent much of his spare time browsing around in Ford's Store, which sold everything from wigs and whale oil to elm bark, brimstone, nightcaps, hoopskirts and tapioca. Ezra Weston's ships brought in East Indian and Oriental luxuries. The assortment of imported goods was the most extensive of any store outside Boston.

The trick, always, is to give the local background to any national news. Thus:

Great excitement in Duxbury in 1765 when the Stamp Act passes. An indignation meeting is held at Town Hall with Colonel Briggs Alden presiding. A committee is appointed to work with other towns for repeal. When news of the repeal came, a celebration meeting was held. After the notables had spoken, the crowd called for Joseph Russell to speak. Although known as the town fool, he gave a witty, impromptu speech.

Another landmark in Duxbury of interest to tourists from all parts of the country is the "Tree of Knowledge." In colonial days, the "runner" between the Massachusetts Bay Colony and Plymouth used to leave messages or letters for Duxbury residents at a large oak tree which stood at the junction of the "Massachusetts Path" and "The Duxbury Road." The tree became known far and wide as the Tree of Knowledge.

With the establishment of the mounted mail carrier, a box

was provided and used during all the years the mail stagecoach made its twi-weekly trips between Plymouth and Boston, thus inaugurating the first "rural delivery" which continued until the railroad succeeded the coach. The tree finally went the way of all earthly things, "when," according to an old account, "to one of the local patriarchs a spirit appeared and warned him, unless the site was marked, a curse would be upon them. So for more than a hundred years, Tarkiln has maintained a sign in memory of the Tree of Knowledge."

When the *Clipper* described this landmark, we received a letter from a Boston banker, who offered to replace the broken glass that shielded the sign that is still read by visiting firemen. The Selectmen took advantage of his generosity.

These are but a few of countless tales interwoven with the history of "olde Duxborough," which also used to be spelled "Ducksberry." None of them can match the story of the late Captain Parker J. Hall, the saltiest character we ever interviewed for *Clipper* readers.

Parker Hall, who died a few years ago in Rockland, Massachusetts at 86, was a veteran seafarer who, except for a black cat or an occasional wife, sailed alone from New York to

Calais, Maine, freighting lumber, fish and gravel. He sailed alone because a two-man crew mutinied on him in Long Island Sound on a July night in 1894.

He loaded and unloaded his vessels unaided, except when the cargo was so bulky the services of longshoremen were needed. Just before Christmas in 1915, when he sailed into New Bedford Harbor in a schooner, en route from Nova Scotia to New York with lumber, he told the folks at the water front:

I can't depend on anyone to handle my vessel just as I want to have her run. Once I had a sailor aboard the old Angler help me run her. It was a clear night and we were going over Nantucket shoals. When we were about two miles from the Cross Rip lightship, I gave the wheel to the man and told him to keep her headed for the lightship. Well, he did just as I told him, and before I knew it, we ran plump into the lightship and nearly sunk ourselves.

While skippering a schooner to New York, he dropped the hook off College Point, Long Island, on the night of July 22, 1894. After a trip ashore, the two-man crew helped him haul his dory aboard. Then, suddenly, they attacked him. Stunned, he pulled out a pistol, shot Frank Duard in the head, and his brother, Charles, in the chest. After Frank died at Flushing Hospital, a jury in Long Island City acquitted Hall the following October.

In his last years, Skipper Hall ran excursions up and down the Maine coast. The son of the keeper of Gurnet Light, he had left home at the age of fourteen. Just before he died, he came to Duxbury, and an old friend of his took us to see him. We found him sitting on a rail fence at the end of Washington Street, near King Caesar's old spar soak. His faded blue eyes were full of remembering.

Back on our porch, Captain Parker Hall, the hardiest skipper who ever quelled a mutiny, rekindled the flavor of old Duxbury for Bobbie and me, and we sat entranced as he recounted salty yarns of Duxbury's most colorful era. Sea captains like Captain Hall were local celebrities in the old days.

Modern Duxbury also has a surprising number of distinguished citizens, some of them more renowned elsewhere than in their own neighborhood. Madison Avenue boulevardiers who think buffalo and coyotes still roam in the small towns of America might like to know that Duxbury is the home of nationally and internationally known persons, many of them listed in *Who's Who in America*.

Madame Elisabeth Weber-Fulop, known for her "speaking likeness" portraits painted with uncanny accuracy, is a former resident of Vienna, Austria, who now lives with her husband Émile (once architect of the City of Vienna) in the King Caesar House. In her Duxbury studio, which once served as King Caesar's slave house, she does portraits that command fees up to five thousand dollars. "Everyone who is anyone has been painted by Madame," said one of her fans. Among her sitters have been Metropolitan Opera star Maria Jeritza, whom she painted three times; August Heckscher, the famed New York philanthropist; Richard Halliburton, the late explorer; former motion picture star Claire Windsor, and the late Boss Ed Crump of Memphis.

Genevieve Thomas, another Powder Point resident, is a sculptress whose figurines are a delight. Her sister, Rosemary Thomas, is a leading poet whose works have often appeared in *The New Yorker*.

Another poet who adds luster to Duxbury is Sarah Wingate Taylor, a descendant of Governor Edward Winslow, and a life-long resident (summer) of Clark's Island, the spot where the *Mayflower* shallop with a party of eighteen men landed in storm and darkness on the night of December 19th, 1620.

Miss Taylor's poems have been published widely, earning her a listing in *International Poetry Who's Who.*

Gershom Bradford is author of a recent book, *Yonder Is the Sea,* and of many monographs on Duxbury's history. His close friend and neighbor, both in Duxbury and Washington, D.C., where they spend winters, is Captain Charles Bittinger, USN. For years, until his retirement, he was the Navy's top authority on camouflage. Captain Bittinger is also a distinguished artist, as are Frank Rogers, Marjorie Billings Andrews, and Marjorie Bush-Browne and Esther Conant, sisters of Dr. James B. Conant.

Although it has been some time since the late Burton Holmes lived in Duxbury, the town has, in Cecil Atwater, a world traveler whose travelogues have won wide acclaim. Atwater, who has lectured all over the United States, is a fellow of the Royal Photographic Society of Great Britain.

Bishop John Wesley Lord is a summer resident, as was the late William Cardinal O'Connell (whose home, Miramar, is now a seminary). Dr. Richard Cattell, who performed the gall bladder operation on Sir Anthony Eden, and Dr. Robert Fleming, founder of the first alcoholic clinic in the United States, who represented this country in an international conference on alcoholism at Geneva, Switzerland, are but two of many distinguished physicians who spend their summers in Duxbury. Another was the late Dr. Emma Erving, a friend of Gertrude Stein's, who was physician for Teddy Roosevelt's children, and those of other Presidents. Dr. Arthur Holcombe, professor emeritus at Harvard University, and former head of the Government Department, was in Switzerland in the summer of 1959 on a UN mission. "I stayed only a week," he told us. "I missed Duxbury too much to remain any longer."

Other interesting personalities who have lived in Duxbury are Justice Felix Frankfurter of the United States Supreme

Court; actress Fanny Davenport and her brother William Seymour, a celebrated actor; "Frenzied Finance" Thomas Lawson, who summered at the Myles Standish Hotel and gave considerable thought to building his "Dreamwold" here in Duxbury before deciding on a manorial site in nearby Scituate (his grandson, Thomas Lawson II, is a resident of Washington Street, Duxbury); Dr. Nathaniel Noyes, well known in medical circles in the horse-and-buggy era, who listed among his patients Fanny Davenport and Adelaide Phillips; and Judge William Thayer, who presided at the Sacco-Vanzetti trial. The murder for which Sacco and Vanzetti were convicted, incidentally, took place directly in front of the Observer-Press in South Braintree, where *The Duxbury Clipper* is printed.

Over the years there has been frequent mention in the *Clipper* of Bobbie's mother, Cid Ricketts Sumner, author of several books of fiction and non-fiction, including *Quality*, filmed as *Pinky*, and *Tammy Out of Time*, which Twentieth Century-Fox screened as *Tammy*, with Debbie Reynolds in the starring role. She was the only woman to take that perilous boat ride down through the rapids of the Grand Canyon from the Green River with the Charles Eggert expedition, a thrilling story she vividly narrates in her book, *Traveler in the Wilderness*. *Clipper* readers were especially interested in her novel, *The Hornbeam Tree*, which opens:

There is a village south of Boston not far enough down to be called the Cape, near enough for rather inconvenient commuting, a typical New England village with green-shuttered white houses, and now and then a gray shingled or a barn-red one with tall elms, lilac hedges and the sea.

If there was any doubt that this typical New England town was dear old Duxbury, Olga Owens Huckins of Powder Point, writing in the Boston Sunday *Post*, dispelled it:

226

No Duxburyite can go to LaFleur's or Josselyn's general stores [she noted in a book review] without hearing somebody ask, "What page of *The Hornbeam Tree* am I on?" or "After Peggy finishes reading it, can I have it next?" Letters of praise or protest are published in *The Duxbury Clipper*. (Mrs. Sumner's travels, her books, her six grandchildren, their parents, and all the relatives that come, part and parcel, to visit her by the sea, keep the social and literary columns of the village paper pretty well stuffed all the time.)

This is but a brief sprinkling of the scores of distinguished citizens whose names make news for the "village paper." The average reader is interested in their activities, and when his own name is linked with theirs in "Around Town," he feels pride in a warm and friendly community.

Do names make news? By themselves, certainly not! If they did, the most fascinating publication in the country would be the telephone directory.

CHAPTER 19

"Measured by all standards, the most I—your newspaper—can hope to accomplish is to constantly improve my coverage, my scope and my services to my community and to my country."

—AMERICAN NEWSPAPER PUBLISHERS ASSOCIATION

Interested in owning a newspaper? The outlook is encouraging, for with the elimination of marginal weeklies, those that have survived command more respect.

The trend toward bigness, in newspapers (think of all the mergers) as well as supermarkets, is creating a new oppor-

228

tunity for weeklies, for with big city dailies increasingly concerned with national and international news, the weekly finds its readers more dependent upon it for news—news of their homes, local politics, education, schools and churches, recreation, club and other social life. The big city daily cannot serve these interests in detail.

Even in metropolitan areas, neighborhood weeklies flourish. There is one in Hollywood that is highly regarded by motion picture stars. Another is *The Villager*, published in New York City. This weekly chronicles the activities of Manhattan's Greenwich Village, whose residents are for the most part Bohemian aspirants to fame in the field of art or the theater. *The Villager* clicks because it chronicles and promotes the specialized traditions of Greenwich Village.

If you think you are otherwise qualified for a career as country editor, but lack sufficient training and experience to launch your career as a publisher, why not get yourself a job on someone else's paper? If you cannot hook onto a big city daily, take an assignment with a small daily or a weekly, and spend a few years learning the ropes. Since, during this period, you will perform many jobs, ranging from reporter to make-up editor, you will richly benefit from the practical experience. An alternative might be to plunge right in, as Bobbie and I did, and learn from, as well as laugh at, your mistakes. You may not have time enough to make all the mistakes we made.

Your aim? You should certainly aspire to make as much money from a weekly as you would working for someone else, but you should not expect to achieve this objective during the first two or three years. Eventually, you should count on earning more money—much more, indeed—than you would if you were a reporter for a big daily.

"If you are a competent newspaperman," said the editor of

a trade journal covering the weekly field, "don't consider going into publishing for yourself unless, after two years, you can be sure of making average 'scale' on a large city newspaper."

"It is a fortunate publisher—and a rare one—who possesses sufficient capital and assurance of success to be able to operate strictly on a newspaper basis," says the government brochure. Sheer nonsense! *The Duxbury Clipper* and other weeklies recently launched in the Old Colony area of the South Shore of Massachusetts obtain most of their revenue from advertising.

If you buy an existing paper, make sure it is a going concern —going in the right direction, that is, mates. An established paper will already have prestige, and advertisers will be accustomed to using its columns. Ask yourself, however, why the current owner wants to sell. Has his paper become a headache? Is the community on the down-grade, or is the paper floundering because of the publisher's personality or ineptitude? If the community looks prosperous and is growing, don't shy away from buying a weekly merely because it is nickeling along as a result of poor management. You may have the talent and industry needed to make it click.

If you decide to buy a paper, how much should you pay for it? One formula is the value of equipment plus gross income for a year. We advise you to avoid buying equipment, if possible, or if you do, sell it and job out your paper. And be sure you and your bride are sole owners. You need no partners to clutter up the premises.

The best opportunities for weeklies are in small towns or rural or suburban areas. Here you will find a captive audience of readers and ideal conditions for a community newspaper. A town of 25,000 may be ideal for a weekly, a town of 10,000 almost as good. But why not a community of 5,000? That's about the population of Duxbury during the winter. No weekly will prosper in any town, of course, unless it fills a need. Swanville, Minnesota, has a population of 373 unless someone moved out or in recently. The *Swanville News,* an excellent weekly, gets by on a circulation of 563, give or take an irate subscriber.

Some of the "do's" and "don'ts" of the profession? First, be sure your advertising rates are high enough to compensate for the cost of mailing, and the loss of revenue that must be reckoned with if you deliver your paper by mail free to your readers.

Encourage your clients to advertise every week, pointing out that the rate for regular advertising is less. If an advertiser tries to sell you the idea that he wants a large occasional ad, show him the value of keeping a one-inch "rate-holder" in the paper at all times at small cost. Charge more for national advertising and for legals. Your rates for political advertising should be at least double, with payment (required by law) in advance.

Your rate for front page ads should be double the "inside" rate.

Collect money for subscriptions in advance.

Drop any advertisers who do not pay within ninety days, and don't be afraid to put advertisers who want a free ride in small claims court. If you don't, word will soon get around town that you are an easy mark.

Hire a country correspondent or two to collect news in the hinterlands and pay them ten cents per column inch.

Use strong editorials regularly to enlighten your readers on community issues and to help them reach proper decisions on matters on which they will vote. Avoid the use of "canned" editorials supplied by syndicates.

Scan the dailies in nearby cities and other papers of circula-

231

tion in your community for news that will interest your readers. This practice, on occasion, leads to unexpected results. Let's imagine we picked up this social note from another weekly that reports some of the activities of Duxbury:

"Last week, Mr. and Mrs. Elmer Doverylittle of Old Cove Avenue drove through Vermont and New Hampshire to see the changing foliage."

The following week the neighboring weekly reprints this breathless news, and the week after that Bobbie, unaware that I have already used the item in the *Clipper*, may pick it up again from the other weekly. By the time the trip the Doverylittles took has been reported for the third or fourth time, the foliage has disappeared, and the leafless trees are somberly silhouetted against a wintry sky.

Use plenty of pictures, despite the expense. Used either alone or in conjunction with a news or feature story, "cuts" will dress up your paper and make it look more professional. Don't worry if there are no facilities for developing and photo-engraving your photographs. We send most of our photos to Florida to be processed. If we are in a big rush, we take them to nearby Brockton for processing. Buy yourself a Polaroid and take shots of local residents and scenes. Group pictures mean more newspaper sales in the stores where your sheet is sold. One resident, photographed with a huge fish he had caught, bought thirty extra *Clippers* to distribute to friends.

Local photographers will supply you with good "glossies," if you give them a credit line under the cut.

Subscribe to *The Publishers' Auxiliary*, the Bible of the country editor. This weekly newspaper is full of hints of good newspaper practice.

Now comes the most important issue of all—the matter of getting as much local news as possible in your limited space.

Brevity, the soul of wit and lingerie, is also the secret of good newspaper writing, which should be concise, clear, forcible, informative and colorful. The princes of journalism, as opposed to the clowns of journalese, often have an arrow-like—even a staccato—style.

A year after *The Duxbury Clipper* made its debut, the Junior Council of Duxbury High School launched a biweekly titled the *Little Clipper*, promoted as an organ that was to record "the activities of the Boy and Girl Scouts and those of the Bon Homme, Myles Standish and 4-H Clubs." It would also have departments on intramural sports, home economics, and drama. "We also plan to run a 'Who Is It?' and a gossip column which, of course," said the co-editors, "will be severely edited."

The "Who Is It?" paralleled the feature running in *The Duxbury Clipper*, while the gossip column was based on "Around Town." When one of the coeditors dropped by to ask for a few tips on running the *Little Clipper*, we mentioned a few writing hints which we later expanded in preparation for talks to students of English at Duxbury High School, and to teachers of English at the annual meeting of the Plymouth County Teachers Association, when our theme was "Teaching Johnny to Write."

Newspaper writing, which can be taught, should combine terseness with vigor. Journalese has been denounced primarily because it too often suffers from a constipation of ideas and a diarrhea of words.

Clarity, logic, and compression add up to style, which is the blood of ideas. Lincoln's "Gettysburg Address" is a good example of the best in style. Eloquence and brevity often hunt in couples. When Samuel Gompers was asked what American Labor wanted, he told the whole story in one word: "More." What speech could have had a greater impact?

The lead paragraph of a newspaper story should outline the whole story completely. All subsequent paragraphs simply add details. That paragraph should have six W's—who, why, where, what, why (or how), and WHOA! It should also have as much color and force as possible:

President Eisenhower, speaking Saturday to fifty Eagle Scouts at the foot of the Statue of Liberty, branded Zeke Stalin, a one-armed deserter from the Russian Army, a liar for saying that most of America's Gold Star Mothers were unpatriotic.

Some country editors write "visitation" instead of "visit," and "collation" instead of "refreshments." Your reader doesn't care what the Little Sisters ate at their annual jamboree, unless the cider gave them hiccoughs and the doughnuts caused seven cases of ptomaine poisoning. And remember that Jane Doe is in charge of refreshments. If they are in charge of her, she should quit drinking.

A country editor should be a leaver-outer, not a putter-inner, since space is a precious commodity. Omit circumlocutions and redundancies. Why say "This involved a considerable consumption of time?" when it takes up considerably less consumption of space to write "This took a long time?" Call that great American dish "hash," not "a conglomeration of heterogeneous, indigestible incompatibles." Here's a sample of purple prose we received: "He accepted the invitation to attend the social gathering at the crowded meeting for the purpose of laying a cornerstone." This boiled down to: "He attended the meeting to lay a cornerstone."

Other inanities include "join together," "few in number," "revert (or refer) back," "settle down," "repeat again," "small in size" and "over with." In each case the first word is sufficient. Happy phrase-makers can be found at copy desks of metropolitan dailies, too. While writing this chapter we paused to glance at the front page of a Boston newspaper looking for a redundancy. We found two in one sentence: "Ralph ——, superintendent of schools in the hilly little mid-Massachusetts town (population: 6,700) swung around in his swivel chair."

Why say "little" if you give the population as 6,700? And why not say that Ralph "swiveled around"?

When we spotted the phrase "general public" in a *Boston Herald* editorial we wrote the editor:

Your editorial writers are not only tops in Boston, but compare quite favorably with the chief editorial writers of some of the weeklies published in the bedroom towns of Boston.

Our ten-year-old daughter, however, has wondered about one of your recurring phrases. She asked us to define the difference in meaning between "general public" and "public." We were unable to answer this question. Will you please oblige?

The amusing reply from the editor:

Certainly. There are all kinds of publics—there is the letter-writing public, and there is the suffer-in-silence public. The general public is just everybody, including editorial writers who use the term "general public" and other editorial writers who point a haughty finger at them. Also including nuisances who compel us to go through a lot of old editorials to see where we used "general public."

At a session at the Breadloaf Writers Conference several years ago, the late Fletcher Pratt, lecturing on economy of expression, was pounced on for using the same phrase—"general public."

After reading some of the garbled copy sent in by some readers, I felt like the college professor who, after correcting freshmen themes all afternoon, drove wearily into a gas station and said, "Hey, chum, amble a few gals of sap into this here old hellskate and don't stand there like you was paralyzed, neither." One person, in a mood nautical, wrote that "all hands were swept off their feet." "Please put this in your classified ads column," another wrote: " 'WANTED: Boy to deliver scallops that can ride a bicycle.' " No town—not even Duxbury—can boast scallops THAT athletic.

In one account, a "stringer"—country correspondent—was listing winners of prizes in the dairy division of a county 4-H fair. After noting that Mary Doe, who had entered a ewe, won a red ribbon for "best grooming," she added that Jane Roe, who had shown a Hampshire cow, won a blue ribbon "for best udders." AND, oh horror, that one slipped by our editorial eye and was printed in the *Clipper*.

When a story contains a long list of names, the *Clipper* gains space by using the "Mmes." or the "Mesdames" title: Among guests were Mmes. John Doe, Thomas Roe, William Hoe. . . ." One of our best correspondents often foils us by dropping a veil of secrecy over the first names of husbands, thus forcing us to write: "Mrs. Annie Doe, Mrs. Mary Roe, Mrs. Hattie Hoe. . . ." At ten cents per column inch the verbiage adds up, but we don't mind that. It's space we need.

When a person dies, he leaves (not "is survived by") a wife, not a widow. Stanley Walker in *City Editor* adds: "His body, not his 'remains' is buried, not 'interred,' in a coffin, not a 'casket,' which in turn is covered with flowers, not 'floral tributes,' while the clergyman (not the 'minister') praises Mr. Doake's good deeds rather than 'pays tribute.' " He further points out that clergymen who are not doctors of divinity should be referred to as "The Rev. Mr.," not as "Rev. Jones."

Remember also, dear and devoted reader, that while a man marries a woman, a woman is married to a man. He is the groom, not the bridegroom, and the bride doesn't wear anything in those wedding write-ups until after she is married.

One moment, PLEASE! What we mean is: she is a bride-to-be, not a bride, until she is hitched.

The country editor, bound by no rigid rules, may ignore some taboos, but if he errs too often his readers will regard him as a rustic gossoon. He can give his paper an individual flavor without sacrificing lucid prose and good taste.

CHAPTER 20

"Fact is, Snoop-Scoop, they is so many things I don't
want or need there ain't enough money nowhere to
buy them if I did. All I want is justice, peace, good
will and my own way."

—The Oldtimer

The Duxbury Clipper celebrated
its tenth anniversary in 1960. It has been a pleasant voyage
so far, and we have made many crossings since this letter
appeared in "Sounding Off" in May of 1950:

Your paper is a welcome addition to Duxbury life. I predict
The Duxbury Clipper will be skimming the Duxbury seas for years
to come, come cross chops or high wind. We have a playhouse
and a newspaper. Now all we need is a bank.

A few years later the *Clipper* noted: "Now we have the
bank. It is another symptom of Duxbury's growth."

Since then, there have been other marks of growth. The
town's water mains are extending into the hinterlands, and
attractive clusters of houses are dotting the countryside. By
1962, the new Southeast Expressway will cut driving time to
Boston almost in half, and Duxbury's sound zoning regulations and protective bylaws will take on an added lure. The
Clipper will be laden with more cargo than ever, for if not
quite so gracefully, it is growing with the town.

Our new *Report from Beacon Hill*, written when the State Legislature is in session by the Honorable Francis Perry of Duxbury, the town's first Representative in more than a quarter of a century, adds an educational note to our pages, and we are happy to note that the *Clipper*, by helping get out the vote, contributed in small measure to Perry's election. Was not some sort of municipal record broken when, in the primaries, he received all but ten votes of the total cast in Duxbury? In the 1952 Presidential election, ninety-six per cent of voters in Duxbury went to the polls—a record only exceeded, and by a fraction of a per cent, by two other towns in the United States.

Even after all these years, Bobbie and I still get a kick out of skippering the *Clipper*, despite critics like the oldtimer, who says:

"Snoop-Scoop, I often wonder whether your news is fit to print or whether it's printed to fit. Don't like the way you change some of the things I say, I don't."

"Oldtimer," your roving reporter said, "the *Clipper* is a family journal. Some of the readers are Brownies and Cub Scouts. In short, some of your spoken remarks are too out."

One satisfaction that comes from running a weekly is having your product appreciated. Blanche White of Washington Street, who has written almost a hundred and fifty *Clipper* pieces, has her own version of the acceptance of a weekly in a community:

In the spring of 1950 when I heard through a tangled grapevine that the John Cutlers were going to start a weekly, I thought it was wonderful and told friends I was going to write for it, even though I did not know Bobbie or John. I knew John as a "voice," having heard him speak at town meeting in a distant corner of the high school auditorium. Actually, it was two years before I started writing for the *Clipper*.

I must have put energy into the job, for in three weeks I got a phone call from John Cutler. He argued that if I had access to so much news, it was my civic duty to see that it reached our Duxbury weekly. I gave the idea a little thought but did nothing about it, and for two years a friendly battle was on.

For me, the going was rough at times, for how the Duxbury folks loved their new little paper! They would be pacing up and down in the Post Office lobby every Thursday morning waiting to get it. I even liked the darned thing myself. I kept plugging away on my column, sometimes convinced that I had only one "constant reader"—John Cutler. I knew he read my column, because every Thursday in the *Clipper* I found four or five items which had appeared in my column the Thursday before. It was still current news to most *Clipper* readers, since few of them read the other paper.

When I started writing for the *Clipper*, I got compliments all over the place from Duxbury readers. You would have thought these were the first words I'd ever written. To a Duxburyite of the 1950's, there was just one paper—*The Duxbury Clipper*.

John took a little liberty with my articles, inserting a line once in a while, knowing I would be more amused than irked. I liked one he used when I completed a school reunion story with a nostalgic *"Tempus fugit."* John added, *"—and non combackum est."* One paragraph I wrote in a piece about a church fair wound up in hilarious juxtaposition to a story John wrote on Duxbury's "turkey row."

John's account mentioned Tony Bongiorno, Nick LaGreca, and John and Joe DeLorenzo, who among them sold almost a hundred thousand turkeys a year. "If all these poultry growers let their hens cackle, roosters crow and turkey gobble-gobble all at once, the din could be heard in surburban Philadelphia," John wrote. Then, immediately following, was a paragraph from my article: "Serving on the board of managers are Mrs. Theodore Chase, Pilgrim Church; Mrs. Everett Handy, St. John's Church; and Mrs. Richard Lewis, First Parish Church." Those turkeys were certainly in good hands!

How quickly, when a useful and pleasant service is introduced to us, and is an immediate success, does it become a way of life.

We forget the beginning struggles and continuing problems of the persons who introduced and maintain this service for us. We wonder what we ever did without our little news weekly which has become such an integral part of our way of life. Never before have so many Duxbury residents known so much about their town government and school affairs, their church functions and the doings of their neighbors. Most assuredly the value of the free publicity given our many worthy projects in this little paper could never be measured in dollars and cents.

As Blanche White implies, there is great satisfaction in helping causes—raising funds for the Little League or Pony League, or plumping for a troop of Sea Scouts until it is finally activated. The *Clipper*, remembering its own upswing days, enjoys helping other businesses to get started or to increase the volume of their business. The West Indies tour of Mr. and Mrs. X, we mention in "Around Town," was arranged by the Duxbury Travel Service, a welcome new enterprise down at Snug-Harbor-on-the-wharf. Many non-advertisers receive "plugs": "Edward Butler, that astute investment counselor, leaves Tuesday for Chicago, where he will study the commodity market." We noted that Roger Griswold of Birch Street makes a complete line of tools for braiding rugs, a unique business, and that Betsy Palmer, Judy Sawyer and Debbie Coffin will "conduct a nursery school this summer." One newsclip from the *Clipper*, scotch-taped onto a cash register of a local restaurant, helped raise funds for a woman left with thirteen children after her husband was drowned. A reminder in "Around Town" may be all that is needed to have a piano donated to a church, and it doesn't hurt when you mention that a blind man makes leather goods for the Village Exchange, or comment on the amazing handicraft sold by The Duxbury Craftsmen. A retired Army colonel suddenly found himself a busy member of the community when the *Clipper* mentioned that he gave excellent illustrated lectures. "And I thought I had retired!" he said. When the American Legion and the ladies of its Auxiliary sent the *Clipper* to Duxbury servicemen, we wrote:

What's new in Duxbury? Well, Dr. Walter Deacon brought home a black bear erased from the Maine wilds, and Ed Sampson, Al Borgeson, and Monty Shirley have dined on venison steaks they didn't buy in any local market. Dr. George Starr stopped shooting ducks when he reached the quota, and the kids have been having fun this schizophrenic winter, picking dandelions one day and picking on their parents to buy them a pair of skates the next day. Boys twelve years old have skated for the first time the same winter juncos have been seen on January second. So few persons have gone to Florida, we are not sending down our mangrove reporter to cover their activities. Wonderful newcomers have moved to town. Train service to Boston is so fast on the new Shoreliner, John Wales started a finesse in a bridge game at Monponsett and completed it just as the train pulled into South Station. Some residents are taking elocution lessons in preparation for a windy town meeting, and everyone, it seems, is on a diet trying to lose the eighteen pounds they gained since they lost fourteen on their last diet. The champion dieter is Bunny Emerson, who has lost sixty pounds. He has lost five pounds on each of his twelve diets, and doesn't five times twelve make sixty? He is as quippy as ever. When I asked, "Have you been entertaining this winter, Bunny?" he answered, "Not very." There were quite a few New Year's Eve shindigs. The population at some of them was larger than the town's total population during the administration of Chester A. Arthur. Nelson Smith is away on another trip. That's it for now, boys and girls, and do let us know what you're doing so we can pass along the word.

It is satisfying, too, to know I make more money from the *Clipper* than I would had I remained a college teacher. Money is not the best thing in the world (the oldtimer says it is better than anything in second place), but it does help rear and educate five children.

242

None of our siblings, however, is impressed by the money-making possibilities, nor do they think the sheet has much social significance. Bobbie and I often wonder whether one of them will take over. "We do have four typewriters, after all," says Bobbie, "and it would be a shame to leave them lying around unused." (One reason I need so many typewriters: Like Truman Capote, who has seven, I have never learned to change a ribbon.)

Robert, who dotes on calculus and analytical geometry, is the least *Clipper*-minded, since he has his sights raised on designing flying saucers, if he can find nothing more abstruse. Ricky, at five, is noncommittal about the possibility of his taking the rudder one day, and Meg, who talks English, Spanish, and back, is tart and aloof when asked whether she'd like to skipper the *Clipper*.

"Oh, for heaven's sake, Daddy."

"I thought you said you wanted to be a writer?"

"I did and I do."

"Then why don't you sail the *Clipper* when you graduate from Vassar? All you will need is a husband who can handle advertising, bookkeeping, housework, and—"

"Because I enjoy writing."

No parent can argue with a sixteen-year-old daughter with flashing brown eyes; he can only give reasons. "Isn't running a successful weekly, newspaper writing?"

"Of course not. Look, Dad, I'm trying to figure out this Virgil person. Why don't you run along. Ask Dave."

Dave rubbed his chin reflectively. "Oh, certainly. I've given the matter of this provincial operation some thought. But I think I'd rather do something more challenging. Maybe go to Harvard Law School or—"

"More challenging? Look, son, running a weekly is even harder than finding a baby-sitter on Halloween. Do you think publishing a weekly in a fast-growing, sophisticated community in an era of increasing competition isn't challenging?"

"Certainly not. What's so difficult about putting out a paper once a week? Anyone can own a weekly. I've heard you say that yourself." There was a note of dismissal in his voice. He was more concerned at the moment with the details of the late Missouri Compromise.

Well, I had to leave, anyway. The damn telephone was ringing, and I could hear Ricky padding across the living room rug. I had to get to the phone first, for if Ricky was in one of his negative moods, he might tell the person at the other end of the line that, nope, it was too late. We might lose another full-page ad or a big story.

Well, Gail, darling, it may be up to you. Ricky has been fooling around with the *Clipper* for at least a year now, and he seems more bored than ever with the routine. Think about it, Gail. It won't do any harm to think about it, will it? After all, the *Clipper* is a valuable property.

Meanwhile, life in a bigger Duxbury goes on. The other day a deer, chased into the bay by a dog, clambered out, lumbered across Washington Street and crashed through a glassed-in porch to interrupt a game of canasta. Then it hightailed off in another splintering of glass while the gentleman of the house phoned his insurance agent. A housewife called to say she had devised a formula that enabled her to determine whether a prospective mother would give birth to a boy or girl, a prenatal concern for some residents of small towns. Two Little-Leaguers pitched no-hitters in the same game (Gene Glass and Billy McNeil), and Gil Francke, a retired business executive, hit a hole in one on the Marshfield golf course. It must be an easier course, since Gil has never had an ace on the Duxbury links.

At the moment, all is quiet along the Duxbury riviera. It's

244

been weeks since we've received a "Dear Sir You Cur" letter, and nobody has thrown a brick through the jalousies. Myles Standish, even though he never commanded an army of more than twelve men, could never have endured the repose. One moment, please. The damn telephone is ringing again. It was Eileen Jones with a little item about a telephone bridge. "Put it on the front page, please," she said. There goes that confounded telephone again. This time it was Philip Delano, chairman of the Board of Selectmen. "There will have to be a special town meeting," he said, "so save a spot for the notice in the *Clipper*. Construction costs have gone up since the town voted that one million three hundred thousand for the new high school. The school building committee is asking for more money." Did I say things were peaceful? Looks as if another storm were brewing.

Bobbie, who just came in with the mail, says she just heard at the post office that a new A & P supermarket will be built at Hall's Corner, another symptom of the town's growth. I hear the wailing siren of the police cruiser. Must remember to check later with the police chief. " 'Bye, Daddy," Gail says. "I'm going to Vicky's birthday party. I'll write down the list of people she invited so you can put it in 'Around Town.' "

The phone rings again. It's a member of the church fair committee. She needs donations for the white-elephant table, she says.

"Write it up in your own words, John," she adds. "Put it on the front page, please."